THIRSTY

SOUL

Finding Rivers of Living Water

All Scripture quotations, unless otherwise indicated, are taken from the Holy Bible, New International Version®, NIV®. Copyright © 1973, 1978,1984, 2011 by Biblica, Inc.™ Used by permission of Zondervan. All rights reserved worldwide. www.zondervan.com. The "NIV" and "New International Version" are trademarks registered in the United States Patent and Trademark Office by Biblica, Inc. ™

Scripture quotations marked NKJV are taken from the New King James Version. Copyright© 1982, 1992 by Thomas Nelson, Inc. Used by permission All rights reserved.

Scripture quotations marked "The MSG Bible" are taken from The Message Bible. Copyright © 1993, 1994, 1995, 1996, 2000, 2001, 2002. Used by permission of NavPress Publishing Group.

Scripture quotations marked TPT are from The Passion Translation®. Copyright © 2017, 2018 by Passion & Fire Ministries, Inc. Used by permission. All rights reserved. ThePassionTranslation.com.

Scripture quotations taken from the Amplified* Bible,
Copyright © 1954, 1958, 1962, 1964, 1965, 1987 by The Lockman Foundation Used by permission." (www.Lockman.org)
Definitions are derived from Merriam-Webster Online Dictionary copyright © 2012 by Merriam-Webster, Incorporated

Interior Design by: https://www.fiverr.com/istvanszaboifj
Asif Cover Design by: https://www.fiverr.com/Designing_Dude
Cover Photo: Nicholas Z. Bell
AMAZON Kindle Direct Press Publishing Platform
ISBN-13: 978-1724267276 (KDP-Assigned)
BISAC: Religion / Christian Life / Spiritual Growth

THIRSTY
SOUL

Finding Rivers of Living Water

KIMBERLY MICHELLE FORD

ACKNOWLEDGEMENT

Heavenly Father, Thank you for being just who you are, for holding my hand when I was lost in the darkness. Thank you for loving me beyond all my imperfections.

My Sweet Jessika, I have watched your cute squirrel cheeks evolve into the beauty of womanhood. You have challenged and defied every obstacle set against you. And in doing so, you showed me, your mom, how to fiercely attack self-doubt and disbelief in my own life. Keep winning Jess—God intends to accomplish GREAT THINGS through you.

Lady Grinstead, Thanks for drawing me into your heart. For charging me to be erected from my places of shame and stand taller. Thank you for your effective prayers and secret wisdom.

Life, thank you for being good to me and for being there every time I wanted to quit.

DEDICATION

For
~Jessika & Karen & Jasmyn~

CONTENTS

Rivers of living water shall flow from
within the hearts of those that believe.
(John 7:38)

ACCLAIM

*F*amily conflict is a topic that many of us are too embarrassed to talk about. When conflict is left unresolved members are left to tackle feelings such as shame, guilt, hopelessness, failure, or trapped. Those broken emotions tend to be passed down from generation to generation. From physical to psychological, family conflict can ultimately diminish our self-worth. Many times, we are left with anxiety and depression –long after time has passed and the members have relocated.

In the Christian community, the church has always been viewed as a place of refuge. It is where many arrive in search of answers and relief from the everyday trials of life. However, quite often, things like emotional distress, family conflict, mental illness, and depression go under the radar in the Christian community. This makes it even more difficult for victims to receive the help they need in order to be delivered. After all, who would want to believe that a person who claims to love Christ would ever intentionally take advantage of others; especially a spouse, their children, or a member of their own family?

The reader of this book will find Kimberly Michelle Ford has skillfully exposed the defining moments of her life. Sometimes our most innocent relationships can become the most significant life changing ones—leaving us broken and unknowingly destined to repeat a vicious cycle. What I find to be most powerful about the message in this book is that: once a person realizes their pattern of destruction, as a result of their own personal choices, new choices can be made.

Kimberly reveals that it is never too late to take your life back. She has confidently learned and teaches others how to speak victory into their situation, by using practical biblical principles. God has promised restoration to all those who will follow them. She shows the reader how self-love is critical when entering into any relationship. In addition, she shares how to overcome shame and guilt – which may discourage individuals from pursuing freedom. In the absence of liberty, we are incapable of beginning the journey towards our unique destinies.

I am excited to hear about the countless testimonies of freedom that will come from reading this book. The anointing of God, which destroys all yokes, is greater than any bondage we may experience. Thank you, Kimberly Michelle Ford, for being brave enough to share your story and the revelatory word given to you by God, to heal all who will read this book. Thank you for helping them to walk boldly out of bondage and into a life of freedom and purpose.

~*Dr. Janet Grinstead*
Puritan Baptist Church
Indianapolis, Indiana

ACCLAIM

*T*he first time I can recall getting to know Minister Kimberly Ford was during a ministry training program in which we both were enrolled in 2010. I am sure our paths crossed prior to that – but nothing that was remarkable. We spent almost two years together in the program. My husband-to-be at the time was also in the program. A few months after our ordination ceremony, my fiancé and I were married. Some time had passed, and I saw Kimberly in the hallway at church. She explained that she came to our wedding ceremony looking for a reason to believe in love again. She expressed how the experience had given her hope. I didn't know the depth of what she meant by "hope" until 2016. At that time, I had created a platform for women to share their stories of overcoming their struggle. I reached out to Kimberly, and she agreed to be interviewed during the event. She began to tell her story and shared some of her most difficult struggles, stretching back to her childhood. As I observed her sharing her story of pain and triumph, I was amazed by her inner strength and resiliency. It was apparent that she had found her way through life. I saw her faith and hope in action, as well as her heart to genuinely help others. Since then, I have grown to respect the work that she does and her passion for serving others.

In this book, *Thirsty Soul: Finding Rivers of Living Water*, you will experience a continuation of Kimberly's work. Her authentic truth and practical examples paint a vivid picture of how one can rise from the ashes of their past. She shares her message with the world because she knows what it's like to be thirsty for all the wrong things. Think about it... there is no feeling like being physically thirsty and not having something to quench that thirst. As for me, I can drink different drinks that are pleasing to the taste buds. A short while later, I will find myself thirsty again. But something else happens when drinking water – an experience that conquers the thirst for good!

Further, do you know that most of the time our bodies are already dehydrated by the time we realize that we are thirsty? Now imagine what it's like to experience thirst in our "soul". In comparison to our physical bodies, *our souls* are already dehydrated by the time we realize that we are thirsty. What would our lives look like if we pursued a deeper relationship with God to quenched that soul thirst –instead of seeking all the things that look good, feel good, and sound good? In this book, Kimberly delivers just how you can do this *–and without judgment*.

As a psychotherapist, minister, and transformational coach, I understand the maladaptive habits that we can come to rely upon when we are seeking acceptance, approval, validation, and love. Our greatest fear as humans is that we *won't* be loved. So, in our fearful pursuit of love, we seek to avoid hurt at all costs. We may find ourselves looking for happiness, peace, and love in all the wrong places. This book offers hope for a path where you thirst no more. Kimberly has shown through her experiences that she has found freedom and she wants the same for everyone else. When we bring our thirsty souls to God's living well, we can have the life of peace, joy, abundance that God intended for our lives.

This process starts with the introspective and reflective practices that Kimberly's words will encourage from the book. You will see her best practices being demonstrated through *her* story. But the truth is, we all have a story that is comprised of our experiences. Every one of your life experiences (the good, the bad, the ugly and the indifferent) have shaped you into the person you are today. It is essential for us to remember that our story does not have meaning, we must *give it* meaning. Beneath the surface of all our experiences, lie a state of completion and wholeness. She reminds us that it is time to awaken to the truth of who you really are – which can only happen by connecting to your source. Your authentic self is enough and when we recognize this –we *thirst no more.* Kimberly has exhibited from her work that despite her flaws –God felt she was still worth forming and has chosen her for such a time as this.

You are not an exception. In every one of us, there is an inner power and strength that is undeniable and "quench thirst worthy". I am thoroughly delighted to recommend *Thirsty Soul: Finding Rivers of Living Waters* to everyone. Please allow the simplicity of this message and its power to transform your thinking and habits. I urge you to pay close attention to Kimberly's message in this book. It will change your life starting right now. Today, you have the opportunity to experience the greater peace, joy, and abundance of God –which ultimately will quench your thirsty soul.

~Minister Natolie Warren, LPC
Atlanta, Georgia

FOREWORD

*I*n this monumental book, Minister Ford walks us through a journey of discovering who we are by first discovering who God is. *Thirsty Soul* works to quench our thirst by correctly filling the voids that we so often feel through lack of understanding. On this journey, you will be enlightened on the great detail God employed as He created and formed the heaven and the earth; that same great precision was used as He created man. Like a flashlight these details will work to illuminate God's intended purpose; His glory.

As you read through each chapter it's essential to note that God uses His voice to pave the way; discerning the voice of God over your own voice creates a way for him to sit down. Minister Ford reveals just that by showing us the importance of our response in laborious seasons. In knowing that God has already mapped everything out; understand this: if He said it, prepare to become able to perform it. *Thirsty Soul* not only helps us to understand the mind of God as He created us but also charges us to walk in the understanding of our potential. Notice how Adam got his compatible mate from the inside of him; understand that God created an environment suitable for us to thrive.

Minister Ford does her audience a great service by revealing and reminding us of our access and privilege to God's power. This is a vital part along the journey to discovery, as it reminds us that God is our source. Not only has He created and equipped us strategically but He shows us that He is with us during every step –by and through His son Jesus. Minister Ford illustrates this knowledge to us by sharing her own life experiences; where her access to God's power became the well she pulled from during her most testing times. From cover to cover, this book works as an instruction manual first by introducing us to our Creator, then by revealing His works through us, and lastly by encouraging us to go forward in strength as the champions we are.

Read on to see what Minister Ford has to say about purpose and its "internal pushing". In her much appreciated and transparent style, Minister Ford reveals how her environments set her up for God's glory to be shown and also to reveal the strength He'd given her. She reveals that through the blood of Jesus she gained confidence to know that she could accomplish all things. For anyone who seeks to quench their thirst through the understanding and knowledge of God this book is your portion.

~Bishop Stephen A. Davis
Newbirth Family Church
Birmingham, Alabama

INTRODUCTION
EARTHEN VESSELS

*G*od *created* the Earth with a treasure hidden inside of it. Our Creator then *formed* the Earth with an extraordinary task in mind. So, get ready at once! Grab your compass, your flashlights, and your maps. Get ready for the greatest quest of your life! Most of us spend our entire lives in search of our unique treasures and assignments. But sooner or later, we all discover that though the *task* is unique to each of us, the *treasure* is universal. We each have a unique assignment to accomplish one distinctive result—His glory.

Imagine this: Earth's sole priority is to replicate His glory. The Earth carries out this assignment by functioning as a vessel which would transport the representatives of His spirit. We are those representatives. You and I represent God's chosen vessels transporting this glorious treasure (His glory) throughout the ages. Think about it. Humanity has successfully carried a treasure that has transcended time, cultures, ideologies, and generations. That treasure has not depreciated over time. Though looking around at the world we live in today, one might believe that God's glory has become irrelevant. One might determine that maybe it has lost its glow. But, I assure you God's glory has lost neither its luster nor its power.

In Jeremiah 29:11, God says "Before I formed you in your mother's womb, I knew you." In this generation, we are finally beginning to understand the depth of the fact that we existed in the heart, mind, and spirit of God before our parents got together and conceived us. Now, time is of the essence for us to fully embrace God's design and order for fulfilling His plan. But, it is critical to understand that we cannot fully embrace God's plan, without first developing an appreciation for the manner in which He created us.

In the beginning, God created the heaven and the Earth.
And the Earth was without form and void, and darkness
was upon the face of the deep.
(Genesis 1:1-2 emphasis mine)

The word "create" in Hebrew is *Bara.* One of the words used to define *Bara* is "choose". That certainly caught my attention. It suggests to me that God had other *options.* Fortunately, He chose the heaven and the earth. Then, I noted that if He had options, there had to be a dilemma to cause Him to consider those options. Now, I am not one to second-guess or question God's intelligence. I am confident that God desired a means to self-reflection. See, self-reflection in simple terms is that act of staring back at yourself, like looking in a mirror.

A few times in Genesis, God shows us how He first creates and then forms that which He has created. First, the term '*create*' shows up in reference to the manifestation of heaven and earth. For several years I was somewhat puzzled when I read Genesis 1:1. I couldn't understand how something could be '*created but not yet formed*'. I think that's a mouthful to begin with.

Isn't it just awesome to consider that God had invested time to imagine the earth (and create it entirely in His mind and heart) before He even lifted a finger to begin to assemble it? My children and I were blessed to have our home built from the ground up. I thoroughly enjoyed the process of selecting floor carpet and tiles, paint colors, elevations, cabinets, etc. When I did the final walk-through in my newly constructed home I was in sheer amazement. Not only was I in love with the seeing the installed options I had chosen. I was also comforted in knowing that the builder had invested the time to carefully planning for this construction—the building in which my life would be lived.

I'd like to imagine just for a moment God sitting there above the heavenly sky, seated in His best meditation pose. Like the Master Architect that He is, God in His preeminence, had created the Earth in His mind and spirit (from conception to complete manifestation) before He gathered the resources to construct it. With His 20/20 vision, He has already inspected every intricate detail of Earth; foundation, lining, center, atmosphere, seasons, substance, and most definitely its inhabitants.

And God said, "Let the waters bring forth abundantly the moving creature that hath life and fowl that may fly above the earth in the open firmament of heaven." And God created great whales and every living creature that moveth, which the waters brought forth abundantly after their kind, and every winged fowl after his kind; and God saw that it was good. (Genesis 1:20-21)

Secondly, we see that God even creates every living creature of the Earth. Let's say He *chose* every being. He decided what animals would roam the earth and what they would be named. He chose their nature. He chose their environment and position on the planet. Some were sent to spend their existence in the air, some were called to exist on dry ground, and some were assigned to exist in the sea. He even chose their means of reproduction upon the earth. He chose their purpose. *Then* He formed them.

So God created man in His own image,
in the image of God created He him;
male and female created He them.
(Genesis 1:27)

And the LORD God formed man of the dust of the ground, and breathed into his nostrils the breath of life, and man became a living soul. (Genesis 2:7)

Then last, but most importantly, God created (chose) you and I. These two scriptures founded God's message to the prophet Jeremiah 29:11. See God was referring Jeremiah back to the beginning of time when he was only a creation in the mind of God. God told Jeremiah in other words, "*I* knew you, before *you* knew you." God's motive, even at that time, was to comfort Jeremiah by reminding him that He invested the required time to meditate on and consider all the details of Jeremiah's life –before He formed him. Being no respecter of persons, our Heavenly Father has done the same thing concerning us. Furthermore, think about this: even your children (and their children's children) *have already been created*.

Right in the midst of the greatest tragedies of my life, God began to speak. While authoring this book, I find myself on the threshold with Jesus—seeking clarity for God's divine order in several areas in my life. While fasting, as I am making my appeal to Him for a full disclosure of His plan, He begins to speak. Finally, He begins to reveal all of the intricate details that are woven into my tapestry.

After surviving my life-altering plunge to 'The Core'[1], I began to recognize the newness of life—the novelty of me (II Corinthians 5:17). I started to understand that it was not *my strength* that propelled me forward when the enemy did everything possible to delay my journey. It was not *my* wisdom, nor was it *my* style. It was not *my* beauty—

---

[1] Source: "The Core – Its All Inside" published August 2007 Author House by Kimberly Jernigan

nor was it *my* strength. It was that which came deep from *within* me; it was my substance.

For thou hast possessed my reins: thou hast covered me in my mother's womb. I will praise thee; for I am fearfully and wonderfully made: marvelous are thy works; and that my soul knoweth right well. My substance was not hidden from thee, when I was made in secret, and curiously wrought in the lowest parts of the earth. Thine eyes did see my substance, yet being imperfect;
(Psalm 139:13-16a)

Now, I must say when David considered that, he definitely had a reason to praise. Just think about it; God knew precisely what He was doing when He created us! Nothing we do takes Him by surprise. He is aware of the things going on in your core. He knows everything happening on the inside of you. He is familiar with the things that you desire, along with the things you fear. He has become acquainted with your tendencies, your weaknesses, and even your strengths. However, even knowing this, He *still* formed you.

Something tells me that God always knew you were worth forming—because of a more significant work which would take place on the inside of you; despite the fears, doubts, and weaknesses. He considered all those things (the things we would typically use to judge and persecute one another) and said, "I still choose him/her;

he/she is still valuable to me". Yes! Regardless of the mess, regardless of your propensity to fail –you are still valuable to God!

Imagine that! Your substance has *value*. God knew precisely what conflict you would face once He formed you. He had a clear anticipation of where you would fall short. But still, God calls you His own because He created something great before He wrapped you in flesh and bones. He created you with His spirit planted inside. When God created man in His image, He knew the *frailty* of man. But still, like stepping into a costume, He chose the *flesh* of man to cleverly disguise Himself. The Lord didn't make the creatures of the earth, or the fowls of the air, or the fish of the sea in His image. He had already chosen man. Let's go back to the beginning again:

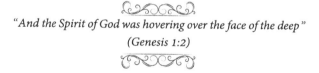
"And the Spirit of God was hovering over the face of the deep"
(Genesis 1:2)

As I carefully watched God, from here (hovering over the face of the deep), to the final formation of man, the Holy Spirit revealed to me that God knew what He was looking for before He even lifted a finger to separate the waters. Let's take this one step at a time. Another word for hovering is *suspended*. I believe that God was *suspended* there for a fundamental reason. As He looked down upon the darkness on the face of the deep, God first spoke the light into existence. Why light? Well, don't you need the light on a treasure hunt – to see in darkness? Then, God separated the waters. Of course, He had to divide the waters. In other words, He ordered the sky to move out of His way and into its position. God was coming after something!

"And God said, Let the waters under the heavens be collected into one place [of standing], and let the dry land appear. And it was so. God called the dry land Earth, and the accumulated waters He called Seas."

(Genesis 1:9-10a)

Now, by God telling all the water to gather into one place, He was ordering the water to move out of the way so that what lay underneath could be revealed. God knew what was there, and He wanted it exposed. God was on an earnest quest for His buried treasure. I am comfortable in saying He was determined in His mission to create this replica of Himself. Once the dry land appeared I would imagine God then took one look at the dirt and was excited about His treasure. He didn't see mere dirt. He imagined much more. He saw Himself. So, He continued from day 3 through day 6 forming everything necessary on the earth for man's sustenance and pleasure. Then in His final creative moment, on the sixth day, He *formed* man – *His image*. I can imagine God saying, "This glory that I have is so marvelous, I have got to see it for myself."

I have been commissioned to tell you that you are no pile of junk. You are no mistake. You are not a worthless failure. You are something awesome. Do you realize that God had Himself (and only Himself) in mind when He created you? He had His own glory –His own power and royalty, in mind when He formed you. If He thinks this much of you, then you should too! This single revelation alone should add value to your own self-image. I know it did for me.

Now that I know what God was pursuing –when He created and formed me, I can endure my journey in confidence. I am fully persuaded that I have the capacity to withstand any test assigned to me. I was in amazement once I discovered that every storm I had ever encountered was designed *especially for me*. Like a tailor-made suit, it would only fit me.

I was at a women's conference a few years back, when I saw a young lady that I knew. I had previously heard her testimony. She stood there in tears as I reached out to greet and embrace her. The Holy Spirit spoke through me, directly to her saying, "You have no idea just how strong you really are." Instantly, I realized that the healing word was just as much for me –as it was for her. God wanted even me to know that everything *I believed* had power over me, indeed held no power at all.

On the contrary, the storms I encountered were there to strengthen me. Like weight training, you never develop muscle until you begin to lift weights. As you carry that

5lb weight, you build muscle, and the fat disappears. But then, it becomes too easy to lift 5lbs, and you stop seeing change. That's when it's time for you to increase the amount of weight you are lifting. In order to continue to see progress in our lives, God will continue to increase the pressure of what we are carrying. But we have no reason to fear. At each level, He trains us for the next.

God could design each storm specifically for me because He knew my unique measurements. He knew He could trust me with these storms because He had already created me with the strength I would need to endure. An enormous amount of fortitude was bestowed upon me at birth. He knew how much He could bend me, and He knew when I would break. So, do you understand that God will only create storms that He knows *you* can conquer? Do you understand that the weight you are carrying right now was only assigned to you? You were formed with all the strength, patience, compassion, and forgiveness to carry your cross.

When we experience tragedy & disappointment, we don't instantly consider how strong God has made us. Instead, we focus on the pain and how bad we want the pain to stop; *immediately*. But if we would begin to look at our *light* afflictions as bodybuilding and not just attacks of the enemy, we would soon discover that we are more than conquerors; we are the replica of God.

So herein lies our problem: we simply are not aquainted with our own strength. So then, God must train us (just like in weight training) to show us what we are made of. See, we never consider going to the next level until we are challenged to pick up the next weight; until we are forced to *raise the bar*.

But there went up a mist (fog, vapor) from the land and watered the whole surface of the ground-- Then the Lord God formed man from the dust of the earth and breathed into his nostrils the breath or spirit of life, and man became a living being.
(Genesis 2:6-7)

I am sure you are already aware by this scripture that you and I were formed with dirt and water; scientifically referred to as *clay*. But have you ever wondered *why* He chose the earth? Well to understand the strength encompassed within our vessel, that is where we must begin. [2]Webster's has two great definitions of clay that inspired me: 1 a: *an earthly material that is plastic when moist but hard when fired* and 2b: *the human body as distinguished from the spirit*.

Upon reading that first definition, I understood that when I, the clay, am placed under fire (the fiery situations in life), I become hard. *Hard* is also described as firm, robust, and durable. That word *hard* is not to delineate the

---

[2] Source: www. M-W.com

arrogant mentality that says, "I am above God" or that, "I am larger than life." But *hard* is to describe the form that I take when placed under fire. Malachi describes that fire best: "*For He is like a refiner's fire and like fuller's soap.*" (Mal.3:3)

We have all experienced the hot seats in life when someone or something is depending on our ability to stand and resist buckling in the fire. Though we stand, we do so not knowing what the outcome will be. But, once we have made the decision to hold our position, God places us down into the fire. With His great hands, He purifies us (as clay) from impure thoughts, motives, habits, and character traits. See, God knows that it is when we are under fire that we will listen to His every word. He knows that at that point we will permit Him to work in us to remove the things that are damaging to our character. And if our attitude is destructive, we lose our ability to witness to the world. Ultimately, His reflection is ruined. I am convinced that God chose to form us of clay (*dirt*) because of our capacity to withstand and thrive in the fire.

When you hear the phrase "Earthen Vessel", what thought immediately comes to mind; the earth maybe? The word *earthen* is simply another word for "clay". But when we focus on the term "earthen", I am forced to acknowledge the apparent parallelism between how God formed me and how He formed the earth. I begin to wonder, "How are we so similar?"

Well, to begin, there are several facts about the Earth's composition to support the idea that when God formed the Earth, He formed it with humans in mind. Like for starters, Earth consists of an iron core that generates a magnetic field. Because of this magnetic field, scientists have studied and found the inner core of the Earth may be rotating faster than its exterior.

Do you know what it feels like to know that something on the inside of you says you are better than your current circumstances? Do you know what it feels like to have a grand vision about your life, then you grab hold of that vision, and you begin to go after it: yet the manifestation of what you envision just doesn't come fast enough? Have you experienced the frustration that comes along with knowing the greatness you see in yourself each night you lie down, in the morning when you wake up, and every spare moment throughout the day; yet you don't understand how to bring it to life?

As I move purposely in this journey, to become that which God has created me to be, I know all too well the effects of the internal pushing and pulling that drives me to bring the things God placed on the inside of me–*to a visible manifestation*. This experience explains the magnetic field God has formed inside each of us.

We are all attracted to purpose. Even though the work required to become who God intended us to be is very frustrating, the force within me continues to move. Just like in the earth, the magnetic field inside of me does not ever reduce its attraction. At times, we can become tired and weary of the obstacles that lie in our path. At times, we may entertain the thoughts of giving up. But, still: the force inside does not stop. It's always ahead of us, pulling us even when we don't want to be drawn. Driving us even when we don't want to be driven; always challenging us. We hear a charge inside of us that sounds something like this: "You were created for something greater than this, keep moving forward! Get up! Get it done!"

[3]*"Scientists also found that the magnetic fields extend infinitely, though they are weaker further from their source. As the Earth's magnetic field extends several tens of thousands of kilometers from the Earth, into space, it is called the magnetosphere. The magnetosphere shields the surface of the earth from the charged particles of the solar wind. It is compressed on the day (Sun) side due to the force of the arriving particles and extended on the night side. A solar wind is a stream of charged particles directly related to the geomagnetic storms that can knock out power grids on Earth."*

Now let's take all of that and apply it to our own human abilities. You have probably at one time, or another discovered that the further you get from God (or the original plan that He set for your life), the more stressed and perplexing the path to success becomes. It is true that we can accomplish almost anything we set our determined mind and strong work ethics to do. We can achieve what

---

[3] Source: www.wikipedia.com –*Scientists also found that the magnetic fields extend infinitely,…"*

would be considered great success in the eyes of man. Unfortunately, all of that success would come with much turmoil, confusion, and possibly manifesting no fruit.

So, just as the magnetic field may run on without end, so do we. And we would likewise become weaker. We, like the Earth, were formed with the highest quality materials. We can achieve great success. But we too, will inevitably become frail, fragile, and exhausted if we move away from our source, our creator, **God**.

But then, even when we stray away from Him, God creates a shield to protect us from seen and unseen dangers that we are too weak and vulnerable to defend ourselves from. I am convinced that God desires for us to learn a valuable lesson from this. Just as the earth's magnetic field is protected by the magnetosphere (because it has moved too far from its source of energy), He also has created an invisible (to man's eye) shield of protection that will divert every arrow and attack (solar wind) sent by Satan to harm you in your state of vulnerability. This invisible shield is what Paul calls the "Shield of Faith".

In addition to all this, take up the shield of faith, with which
you can extinguish all the flaming arrows of the evil one.
(Ephesians 6:16)

We only recognize that the shield exists when we are susceptible to attack. It is when we are faced with certain death, possible defeat, or injustice that we are forced to tap into the strength found at the core of our being. We are challenged to remain erect despite potential demise.

I like the fact that the article also states that "the Earth is compressed on the day (*Sun*) side, but then extended on the night side." Compressed means to be: *trodden, crushed, or trampled.* What God is saying to me is that when the sun shines in my life, and when things are going well; it is then that He allows me to be trodden, crushed, and trampled upon by people, emotions, and anything that would bring me to my knees in prayer. It is during this time that the force of the arriving storms (*solar winds*) causes me to be compressed and then prepared for the night time.

To be extended means to be: *unlimited or boundless.* In our night times (or the dark moments) we find out that we have more unexplainable love to give. It is then that we forgive beyond measure. It is during our darkest seasons that we are *challenged to defy the od*ds. The "night time" provides an opportunity for us to learn just how free (boundless) we are to go above and beyond what is required, for the sake of the gospel. In this dark season, we are introduced to the infinite power within us to reach the lost.

Furthermore, I'd like to say that the "night time" in our lives will reveal to everyone what we have spent the *day* doing. Have you spent the day praying, studying God's word and applying His principles? If you have, then during the night time (when we are attacked, when things happen in our lives that would typically cause us to break) our responses to these tragedies will reveal how God has perfected us behind the scenes. How about that?!

Naturally, we are not happy when these strong winds occur; nor do we enjoy the force of impact upon us. No one in their human nature would respond to death or tragedy with celebration. But if we surrender (and let God do the work He needs to do in us), they will prepare us to withstand greater challenges later down the road on our journey. These moments will also prepare us to be a light –illuminating the path to freedom for others. You may be surprised at how your demonstration of resilience, may provoke strength in someone else's dismal season.

But in a great house, there are not only vessels of gold and of silver, but also of wood and of earth, and some to honor and some to dishonor. If a man, therefore, purges himself from these, he shall be a vessel unto honor, sanctified and meet for the Master's use, and prepared for every good work.
(II Timothy 2:20-21)

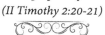

Here in II Timothy, Paul addresses the new leader, young Timothy. Paul expresses to him just how important it is to keep himself in good shape for the work of God. He told him to cleanse himself from everything that would dishonor his position with God.

See, in order to be useful for God's work, He will test us. The testing is to eliminate anything that would disqualify us from being fit for the battle over His kingdom.

Furthermore, the tests will not end until we are purified of every toxic relationship, weak thought pattern, and destructive habit. We are simply not prepared for *any* of God's work if we have not been proven resilient.

God's way of purging us (which is to remove all those things that are a detriment to our success), is by subjecting us to a series of tests and trials that reveal our weaknesses. Anything that does not reflect the likeness of God Himself will only hinder our progression. When God is purging us, He tests our ability to give. He examines our ability to forgive, to love, and to stand under pressure. And each time we are presented with an opportunity to choose God's way, we should (by all means) give Him our best.

When we fail Him, we are forced to go through that same drill again and again—until we pass. Take note that passing never implies that you have "arrived". Passing demonstrates that you have accepted His way and have given up your will for His. Once the principle is deeply rooted in you, then you proceed to the next learning curve.

When God sees that you have incorporated His principles into your lifestyle, He releases you into the next level of your destiny. But I must remind you that destiny is not just a place, like the Promised Land. Destiny is not an event or an accomplishment, like a wedding or a graduation. Destiny is a *responsibility* to fulfill. Once we discover destiny, that responsibility becomes our motivation to get up out of bed every day. Destiny becomes our reason for living.

It is during the night time when we are affirmed and prepared for *every* good work. Not just *some* of the work; but *every* good work. If we do not complete the drills and instead remain rebellious against God's refining process, we are living in vain according to God's standards. And this is the part that frightens me at times: God has full autonomy to destroy that which refuses to belong to Him. He is truly sovereign in that respect. But because He loves us with an eternal love, He wants the best outcome for each of us. He has it all planned out –for our good! And His plans are simply marvelous! He believes in our success. He is confident that we are capable of great things! He gives us chance, after chance—after chance. After all, He made the most significant investment in you than anyone ever will. He invested *Himself.* And that's where His confidence lies!

Yes, God raised jesus to life! And since God's Spirit of Resurrection lives in you, He will also raise your dying body to life by the same Spirit that breaths life into you!
(Romans 8:11 TPT)

"But we have this treasure in earthen vessels,
that the excellence of the power
may be of God and not of us.
We are hard pressed on every side,
Yet not crushed;
We are perplexed, but not in despair;
persecuted, but not forsaken;
struck down, but not destroyed—
always carrying about in the body
the dying of the Lord Jesus
that the life of Jesus also may be manifested
in our body."

2 CORINTHIANS 4:7-10
New King James Version

...so that the Excellency of the power
may be of God, and not of us.
(2 Corinthians 4:7)

1

EXCELLENCE OF POWER

ust how well do we understand the "*power*" that has been granted to us? We do know that the power of "*God*" was bestowed upon us through the sacrifice of Jesus Christ, right? Not the President, the Pope, or the Queen of England. But the unmatchless power of "*God*"—our divine and sole Creator of the heaven and earth. However, when we examine how many of us live our lives under the shame of inferiority, how many lives are lost to senseless tragedy, and how many battles are fought over material success –it is very clear that we lack understanding of the divine power we possess.

Yet, we should also take into consideration that had it not been for the sacrifice of Christ, we would still be a creation of weak, hopeless people, with no access to redemption. There would be no supernatural signs or wonders to experience. There would be no healing power in our hands. Furthermore, the words we speak would lack power. Had it not been for Jesus' willingness to suffer (while others enjoyed the luxuries of this world), and the power granted to us in his resurrection, we would be a species of ineffective people. We'd find ourselves scrambling through our experience on earth –searching for a hint of evidence that we are not *alone*.

Do you understand that since God is with us, that we have *access to* and *privileges of* His power? I would be the first to tell you that because of His presence, we have the key to unlocking every area of our lives that has been bound. Imagine that! So many people spend their entire lives oppressed. Yet if only they knew; they indeed possess the keys to set their own souls free.

The same redemptive power demonstrated at the cross empowers me to view my past through the eyes of victory. It is also because of that power that when I look back and reflect upon my history, I can hold my head up and smile; knowing that despite my experiences I can still give God credit for every obstacle I overcame. That may sound cliché. But I must warn you; it is far from christian rhetoric. Giving God the glory is declaring to the world, "Even though I suffered abuse, rejection, and neglect, I thank God for it. I would not be *who I am* and *where I am* today without those experiences". You will only hear that type of praise from someone with an amazing amount of spiritual maturity.

Life and death only occur by the power and will of God. Therefore, it should be clear to each of us, that each time Jesus raised the dead, God was offering us the *evidence* our human minds would need in order to believe that His presence is indeed *with us*. The moment Jesus completed His season in the wilderness, God began to perform a plethora of miracles to prove that He is *with us*. Jesus even reminded his *nay-sayers* on occasion that, "I only do what the Father wills me to do." Yet sadly, even the disciples continued to request more evidence.

I am wholly convinced that even as Jesus endured the lies, betrayal, and torment from those he was sent to save, and wept on the outside –at the same time on the inside, he rejoiced. His rejoice came from the wisdom in knowing this: even though the enemy planned to have Jesus killed to hinder God's work, instead Satan had *unintentionally* enabled the gospel of Jesus Christ to be born.

> *Behold the virgin shall be with child and bear a Son, and they shall call him Immanuel, which is translated, "God with us."*
>
> **Matthew 1:23 NKJV**

See, when Jesus showed up at Satan's doorstep (after the crucifixion) and snatched our freedom from the enemy, Satan realized he'd made a terrible mistake! He had done just the opposite of what he intended. His goal was to destroy God's plan to redeem mankind. Yet instead, God used the enemy's plan to make the most important move of all (by betraying Jesus to the Romans). This one move alone set Christ's 3-day journey in motion. This move would catapult him to his most defining moment here on earth. I can imagine Jesus arriving in Hell after his crucifixion with a smile on His face and a laugh in his heart; knowing He indeed had the victory. Satan's ignorance granted Jesus just the access he needed.

Had the enemy not inspired the Pharisees and Sadducees to demand the murder of Jesus, Jesus would not have obtained access to enter the gates of Hell. But he knew that to retrieve the keys to life and salvation for all of mankind, he would have to suffer. Though he had no experience with sin, he would have to suffer *and die* like a criminal. Jesus knew his own death would grant him access to the enemy's assembly room. He understood *why* and *how* he had to die. So, he came on the scene prepared. His greatest sorrow was that his family, the disciples, and even those who killed him, could not fathom that it was all for their good.

Verily, verily I say unto you, unless a grain of wheat falls into the ground and die, it abideth alone; but if it dies, it bringeth forth much fruit."
(John 12:24NKJV)

When you plant a kernel of corn what grows at harvest time; an ear of corn right? And as the scripture says, that ear produces many more seeds. If Jesus had stayed, defended himself, and avoided the crucifixion, he would not have fulfilled his mission to replicate the glory and power of God on the earth. Remember, the name Immanuel means: *God with us.* I know some people have a hard time receiving this, but Jesus was God-wrapped in a body of flesh –born with the sole intent and purpose of

42

dying –so that He (God himself) would reap a harvest of souls that would replicate Him. God was the first initial seed. Do you understand what that means? We are truly missing the boat when we don't realize just how much power we *already* have.

Each opportunity that we get to stand in the shoes of Jesus (when we are persecuted, lied on, rejected, and imprisoned), we are afforded the chance to manifest and exercise the power of God within us. This reminds me of a situation I experienced many years ago. A particular young woman alleged that I had stalked her and harassed her by calling her repeatedly and hanging up the phone. I was also accused of stalking her by mysteriously driving by her home at night. This woman requested a warrant for my arrest, and I was forced to appear in court to defend myself.

Now the truth of the matter was that my daughter witnessed criminal activity while visiting her home. I was obligated to report the incident to local authorities. Unfortunately, as a result of my attempt to protect my children, 3 months later in return, I was served a subpoena. Amazingly, this young woman fabricated a story and was willing to lie to authorities. I recognized the motive driving all of this was her need to punish me for the pain she felt in her relationship; this was her revenge. Have you ever heard that hurting people hurt people?

I was instantly amazed at the lies as I stared at the accusations in the warrant. At a loss for words and dumbfounded, I could not understand how someone could dig so deep to fabricate such a massive lie. This, I knew was the work of the enemy—the father of all lies. Though at the time, I could not afford to obtain legal representation–I never entertained fear. I actually thought it was comical. My husband thought I should take it more serious than I did. But the truth I knew in my heart was much more potent to me, than what I read on that piece of paper.

I knew that I was a child of God, and He has plans to prosper me and not hurt me. I knew that He would not allow the enemy to be successful with any of his weapons against me. Furthermore, I knew that because I had been placed in the fire unjustly, that the power of God was about to be manifested through me. I became excited, because I knew that I already had the victory.

You prepare a table before me in the presence of my enemies. You anoint my head with oil; my [brimming] cup runs over.

(Psalm 23:5 Amplified Bible)

I contacted my phone carrier and had them to send me a full report of every number I dialed for 3 months straight. This was the only evidence I would have to prove that I had no interest in contacting the woman. So, I gathered all my documents and asked a relative to come with me and stand by my side for support.

Pilate, therefore, said unto him, "Art thou a king then?" Jesus answered, "Thou sayest that I am a king. To this end was I born, and for this cause came I into the world, that I should bear witness unto the truth. Every one that is of the truth heareth my voice." Pilate saith unto him, "What is truth?" And when he had said this, he went out again unto the Jews, and saith unto them, "I find in him no fault at all."

(John18:37-38 nkjv)

We stood at the courtroom door waiting for my name to be called when my relative saw a friend of hers (who happened to be a lawyer). She spoke with him briefly and asked him to represent me. After carefully examining my documents, he asked me one question, "Is there any way my accuser could possibly have any evidence supporting her allegations?" My answer was a resounding, "NO." He replied, "Let's roll." At that moment, I was excited to see God work!! I knew without a doubt that the Holy Spirit was with me. He would surely guide me into ALL truth.

As I sat there listening to the lies being told, it was fascinating to witness someone stand in a court of law and justice –then blatantly lie. To this day, I still get tickled when I think about the whole story. I wondered just how broken one's soul must be to plan and then carry out such an act. I asked myself, "Doesn't this woman have a trigger in her soul alarming her that what she was doing was wrong? Wasn't there any conscience? Wasn't there any personal conviction? The answer was "no."

At this moment, I remembered Jesus and how he endured the same injustice as the Jews sent Him before Pilate and surrounding courts looking for someone to validate their lies. They, likewise, sought the imprisonment of Jesus and even more demanded his Crucifixion. When I remembered this, I took honor in the fact that I was not alone.

God makes no mistakes when His people are in trouble. When God delivers His people, *He goes all out!* His miracles can be compared to baking. You know how you can always taste the difference between frozen pizza filled with preservatives and pizza made fresh from scratch? In a gourmet pizza, you can seemingly identify each ingredient individually. Let me say this: God makes sure that He takes the time to carefully consider and select each element for your miracle to take place. He goes to great lengths to reveal Himself in our lives. He develops a strategic and precise method for demonstrating His power. When we are blessed to witness Him at work, we are left in sheer amazement. We proclaim to everyone we know in excitement—"Only God could have done that!!"

I initially planned to come to court and testify to the truth in my own power, my own words, and my own strength; of course, while knowing that God was with me. But let me explain what God had in store because of my faith in *His power*. I must tell you, He really exceeded my expectations of Him that day. As I waited, my lawyer revealed to me that this judge is his neighbor. At that moment, my confidence grew further. My name hadn't even been called yet—but I was already recognizing God's hand of favor orchestrating a miracle on my behalf in the courtroom. I knew that I didn't have to do or say anything else. It was as if I immediately saw His signature on this victory. He had it all under control. Now, I could have been so prideful and not asked my relative to come along with me. But then, I would not have had access to *this* lawyer –*this* lawyer who had favor with *this* judge.

Well, the judge gave the woman the opportunity to voice her reasons for requesting my arrest. She accused me of driving past her house several times unannounced. Yet she could produce no evidence that this had occurred. Her next accusation was that I called her several times and hung up. Her only evidence was that her caller ID read "Private Number." The judge allowed her to say all she had to say. She then turned to my lawyer. I was asked three questions: Did I call her? Did I drive past her house? And when was the last time I spoke with her? After clearly stating the truth, the case was immediately dismissed.

Though my relative and I left there laughing, I hadn't said anything more to the young woman about it since the incident. I never exposed or gloated to her how God's hands had moved on my behalf that day. See, her goal was to attack me with public humiliation. Yet instead she got just the opposite and left there humiliated herself. Even my relative said to me with a smile, "God always has a ram in the bush." Apparently, my enemies learned just how much God loves me and how He would protect me that day. The enemy had come in like a flood to surround me. But in response, God lifted a standard against the attack. That standard was TRUTH. I witnessed an overwhelming manifestation of God's power in the courtroom that day. It remains a testimony I will never forget.

"I have given you the authority to trample on snakes and scorpions and to overcome all the power of the enemy; nothing will harm you."
(Luke 10:19)

After witnessing God's hand move like this, I began to experience a level of confidence I had never felt before. I know that it will never be because of my own efforts, ideas, or the human psyche that I will succeed at anything. Yet, I am more than able to accomplish *all things* by the power we received by the outpouring of the blood of Jesus Christ. His blood acts as a protective covering which is invisible to the eyes of the enemy. So, he will foolishly continue his attack on us and run into a wall, harming only himself every time.

Because of the blood, I have the power to dance on the head of the enemy, diffusing every flame he lights for my footsteps. Though he expects to see me stumble and fall, I can still walk forward with my back straight and strong. I can move forward with my heart filled with faith that I have *already* overcome. I can sprint ahead towards every battle with confidence that my opponent is already defeated.

Nay, in all these things we are more than conquerors through Him that loved us. For I am persuaded that neither death, nor life, nor angels, nor principalities, nor powers, nor things present, nor things to come, nor height, nor depth, nor any other creature, shall be able to separate us from the love of God which is in Christ Jesus our Lord.
(Romans 8:37-39)

Look at these two simple word equations:
Christ Jesus = Access to the Love of God
The Love of God = POWER

Paul conveys to us in Romans 8:37-39 that: *It is through the power of the blood of Jesus Christ that we are able to overcome every trial and attack sent by the enemy.* The equation above tells us that if we have Christ Jesus in us and make Him a part of our everyday lives, then we have access to the love of God. Then, once we experience the unconditional love of God, we come in contact with and begin to recognize that we actually possess His *power.* Paul wanted his readers to grasp the idea that no matter what prison he found himself in, no matter what judge he stood in front of, and no matter how bad the persecution he would suffer, the blood of Jesus Christ gave him the power to withstand it all! And his knowledge of that power gave him confidence that he would never suffer *alone*. Once you accept Christ Jesus, you have access to a force that will see you through *anything*—and that power is *the Love of God*!

> *Whoever denies the Son does not have the Father either; he who acknowledges the Son has the Father also.*
>
> *(1John 2:23 NKJV)*

That same truth should remain with each of us. You may have lost a job, suffered the death of a child or spouse, lost a marriage in divorce, or endured public humiliation. But God wants you to always be reminded that you are not alone. You didn't just receive His son into your life, but through His son you have Him. Yes, that's right! You have the power of God Himself residing in you. Did you actually think Jesus came just for you to receive him and get saved from a burning hell??? That's a very important aspect of salvation, but that isn't the *only* reason he died. He ultimately came to reconnect us back to the Father. He not only came so that we may have victory in eternity, but also in our everyday lives.

When sin arose in the Garden of Eden, humanity was immediately disconnected from its source of power; God. But once we fully receive Jesus, we are immediately plugged back into the power source. Once we are reconnected back to that power source, nothing can separate us from His power. I am convinced it is because, once we plug in, God won't let us go. Ahhhh, yes! That's why John says, "Greater is He who is in me than he who is in the world."

I believe that once Paul plugged into the power source on the Road to Damascus, and once God got a hold of Him, no matter how much pain he felt on the surface – the love, joy, and peace that resonated from within him were much more significant. Now here's a thought for mature thinkers: In everything we do, we should approach it with excellence. Yet, whatever we pursue, it will never be our best unless it is initiated by Him—through us.

"And be not conformed to this world: but be ye transformed by the renewing of your mind, that ye may prove what is that good, and acceptable, and perfect, will of God."
(Romans 12:2)

We are hard pressed on
every side, yet not crushed...
(2Corinthians 4:8 NKJV)

We've been surrounded and battered
by troubles, but we're not demoralized
(The Message)

2

NEVER QUESTION
THE PRESSING

---

ost of us can relate to the term *'hard-pressed'*. In Hebrew, it is: afflicted, bruised, pierced, distressed, broken, discouraged, and broken down. The word *'hard'* informs us that the manner in which we are developed is rough; it's not an easy going, comfortable pressing. It hurts! When we hear the words *hard-pressed*, we automatically associate it with pain, discomfort, lack, or some form of ill-treatment. While it is true that being hard-pressed does include all of the above, I wonder: do we really understand the message Paul was desperately trying to convey to us as he wrote this line in Corinthians? Have we undoubtedly gathered the strength he imparted to us; being "hard-pressed on every side- *and yet still not crushed*?

His words imply to me that to be hard-pressed is a painful position. And to remain uncrushed demonstrates our willingness and our capacity to endure our blistering and painful situations without caving in. It implies that I can stand on the brink of utter destruction and still *expect* to see victory. I can face what may appear to be an inevitable failure; yet in tandem, have a firm grasp on HOPE.

> *"These things I have spoken to you, that in ME you may have peace. In the world you will have tribulation; but be of good cheer, I have overcome the world."*
>
> *(John 16:33 NKJV)*

Quite naturally, this is not a position anyone in their human or carnal mind would intentionally subject themselves to. On the contrary, it is quite natural that we would all strive to live a life of peace and tranquility; a life free from chaos, disappointments, rejection, and worry. However, I am confident in saying we have all discovered one way or another that no matter how hard we struggle to shield ourselves from trouble, it remains a never-ending battle. As we continue to have breath in our lungs, various trials will rampage through our lives (as if our tests could pick their victims). Until the return of our savior, *turmoil and conflict will exist.* Jesus was even sure to make it clear to us that *"In this life, ye shall have tribulation."(John 6:33)*

In my first book, "The Core: It's All Inside", I encourage readers to take the time to seek out the personal, internal obstacles that destroy fruitfulness and then find the will to demolish these strongholds. In that book, we learned that as we journey to *The Core* in search of our true selves, we also unveil hidden forces (like abandonment, insecurity, rejection, etc.) that refuse us access to live. Upon our discovery, we develop courage by going against all the odds and dethroning these forces and their false sense of power. Here, I must inform you that it can be surprising to find out that victory over our strongholds only prepares you for something much bigger: *Life*. After your core experience, it is imperative that you understand this is when the real pressure begins. Yes, God has been with you all along, and that contributed to your victory. And yes, you surely possess the territory in which you were created to reign. You have taken back everything *you thought* the enemy had stolen. However, I am sure you can identify with the truth that you are still not exempt from pressure.

I know all too well what it feels like to have every area of my life challenged by storms. Shall I paint the picture? Let's say one of your kids is not doing so well in school, you despise the husband you once adored, and he rejects you more than he romances you. You wonder, (probably more than you will openly admit) "What is this *thing* I married?" You feel that your boss is an agent from Hell who's threatened by your intelligence and her only goal is to back you into a corner to fail; you endure her scoffing remarks and condescending behavior. Still, regardless of how often you cower down and feed her ego, you're always one step away from the *'tap on the shoulder'* and a pink slip. Tension rides your back each day because you're living from paycheck-to-paycheck and can't advance beyond being one paycheck away from the homeless shelter. You have great big dreams! And you envision yourself enjoying a quality of life so much sweeter than your current reality. You've discovered and embraced your purpose; you would do anything to arrive at destiny. You are ready to experience the type of life you've only heard of: waking up to live, instead of waking up to work. If only you could pursue the things you are passionate about full time! However, it appears that unforeseen circumstances continue to tell you: "*Access Denied.*"

[4]*Every day offers a chance to choose anger or understanding, bitterness or acceptance, darkness or light. And the choices we make undoubtedly reveal the stuff we're made of.*
–Robin McGraw

Let's take a look at the mathematical explanation for our troubles. Look at that word *'circumstance'*. The whole word is the present participle of *circumstare* which means to stand around. It's made up of two parts *circum-*

---

[4] Robin McGraw-*excerpt from* From My Heart to Yours: Life Lessons on Faith Family and Friendship

(around) and *stare* (which means to stand). We can learn a lot about our circumstances, if we go to the word circumference. The general definition of *circumstance* is: the sum or total of essential and environmental factors. These factors are the events and situations that surround our lives –individually and collectively (i.e., the state of our economy, your job status, your health, your financial stability). Our circumstances may consist of several issues like debt/poverty, lack of efficient transportation, and disease. Well in comparison, the general definition of the word *circumference is*: the total distance around the outside of a circle.

Let's talk about the diameter. The general definition of *'diameter'* is- a straight line measuring from one side of a circle directly across to the other side. If you think about it, we can go through a whole 365-day year and encounter countless tragedies, failures, and disappointments. That line represents time spent in prayer,

Jabez called on the God of Israel, saying, "Oh that you would bless me indeed and enlarge my territory, that your hand would be with me, and that you would keep me from evil, that I may not cause pain!" God granted him what he requested.

1Chron. 4:10 NKJV

worrying if we will ever find relief; yet still evolving from conflict to resolution.

The spiritual definition of diameter is: our ability to reveal to others what we are made of – our substance. The diameter exposes our true character; the attitude exhibited as we are waiting for God to elevate us from poverty to wealth, to promote us from shame to vindication, to move us from grief to joy, or to heal us from sickness back to health.

The total of all that we experience is our circumference, but the energy which we give these experiences is considered *our diameter*. Another word for diameter is 'width'. So, let me ask you this: what is the diameter (or width) of your life? How long does it take you to grow from feelings of fear, complaining, and embarrassment – to feeling confident, humble, and spiritually mature? How often do you repeat the same tests, and travel around the same mountains –simply because you refuse to surrender to God's blueprint for your life?

A prime example of an individual in tune with his diameter is Jabez. His very name meant 'pain'. We don't know what aspect of pain this mother experienced. But I can imagine it must have gone beyond the typical pains of childbirth. It is natural for any mother on the delivery table to instantly forget the pains of childbirth once she lays her eyes on the blessing. Ladies, I know we could swap neverending delivery room stories about the pain of our contractions and our experiences in triage. But men, after nine months of carrying this weight, excruciating back pains, and sleepless nights –in that moment of relief, the last thing we think of is "pain". All we can focus on is the blessing staring back at us with an innocent gleam of hope. We think "What joy it is to behold God's creation! This is what I have been waiting for!"

So, for the mother of Jabez to only conjure up the word "pain" at the sight of her child I am compelled to consider that her pain had very little to do with the child-birth activities. I believe there was so much more going on in her life that her emotional distress would not allow her to enjoy the priceless moment of holding her new-born baby.

Her pain could have derived from financial strain, emotional distress, loneliness, homelessness, the exile of her people, or the abandonment of Jabez's father. We don't know precisely what caused her such agony. At any rate, we have a baby boy destined to grow up with a name he would always hate. This very name and the pain associated with it is what led him to pray the infamous prayer including this notable appeal: "*enlarge my territory.*"

"Enlarge my territory" is a request suggesting to us that Jabez lived a life stifled by limitations. A life filled with what may appear to be never-ending limitations will eventually result in a hope deficient life. Jabez had experienced the hard-pressed life Paul described. Think about it. If someone is in distress and confined to their dire circumstances –isn't that a demonstration of hard-pressed? Jabez lived a '*hard*' life, and he was '*pressed*' within the confines of his limitations. We can also say that Jabez was suffocating or felt trapped in his unfortunate circumstances. As a result, Jabez was driven back and forth (and sometimes in circles) in pursuit of an opportunity to alter his identity. He desperately desired to make his mark in the earth despite his reputation. Instead of being identified as the boy who brought *pain*, his mission became having an impact that would cause people to associate him with *honor*.

I believe Jabez ran until he was tired of running; until he ran out of options and ideas. All he knew at this point was to call upon the Father from above and nearly demand that he be granted more time, more influence, *and more insight.* His sincere outcry and deeply rooted passion for a new beginning, brought God the acknowledgement He deserved. As a result, God was able to carve the image He originally intended for Jabez. This one prayer caused Jabez to peak in His relationship with God. Jabez's willingness to *surrender* is an indication that He had run as far as he could on his own and had now reached the most critical moment in His relationship with his Creator.

Once Jabez surrendered, God could show him new opportunities and challenge him to pursue the impossible. It wasn't that Jabez had been given more money or clothes than he already had. But God expands his mind to the point that Jabez can see unlimited possibilities. The glass walls and ceilings were no longer in sight, and suddenly Jabez became aware that he had *access*. Fervent prayer and consistent communication with God transforms Jabez's self-perception; he now sees himself as God sees him. He no longer surrenders to limits; he is now empowered to pursue all the *possibilities*!

Just like Jabez, in your diameter (place of substance) I am sure you have been driven back and forth (and sometimes in circles) from one issue to the next in your life looking for answers; undoubtedly chasing the life God has shown you in your quiet time with Him. Yet you may feel that you are only ending up at the circumference (total) of your life and thinking, "Okay here is another endpoint (roadblock), I'll just go in another direction." And you do this aimlessly back and forth not knowing if you will ever reach destiny.

Let's go back to our circle. The *radius* is the distance from the center to the perimeter of the ring. In mathematics, we are taught that if you know the radius, you can always find the diameter; just because it is always twice as large. I would like to present a thought here: the diameter (or width) also represents your circle of influence, your resources, your ground to work; your territory. Remember, the general definition of circumstance is: *the sum of essential and environmental factors (as of an event or situation).*

And He said unto me, "My grace is sufficient for thee: for my strength is made perfect in weakness." Most gladly, therefore, will I rather glory in my infirmities, that the power of Christ may rest upon me.

(2Cor.12:9 NKJV)

So, let's look at the circle below. Notice that circumference is on the outer perimeter of the circle; remember this is just another word for your *circumstance.* The center is where you S-T-A-N-D. This season is where you can't see how you will make it through, but where you must hold on to faith and stand in the middle of the storm. This is also the moment when you recognize prayer is non-negotiable. Here, you find solace as you and Christ walk together hand in hand with the Holy Spirit as your guide. The middle of the storm is where you must learn not to grow weary while you know you are doing the right (most times unpopular) thing. The center is where you live in peace and trust God to provide for your every need—emotionally, physically, financially, socially, etc.

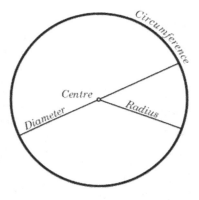

The radius is the distance between you and it. *"It"* is the sum total of your experiences. This radius is the distance between you and how you manage the problems you face on a daily basis. This range represents just how much energy you spend worrying about bills, the kids, your degree, the promotion, your marriage, your divorce, your home, etc.

We have all heard the phrases, "the bigger the storm –the bigger the blessing", and "the higher the level –the greater the devil". Well here is the mathematical equation that supports those ideas: your diameter = radius x 2.

Do you recognize that as the diameter (width of influence) increases the circumference grows even greater? As your influence increases, your territory increases, and your circumstances are multiplied. There are more relationships to manage, and there is a greater responsibility to deliver. The circle grows wider!

See when opportunities for advancement increase, we discover what people are truly made of. And if you pursue more than you have the capacity to manage, your inadequacies will be exposed. So, it is important to tread lightly as we seek to go to higher heights. It is imperative that we seek God in prayer to determine if we are in alignment with His timing and His will for our lives. We will not be prepared for every single opportunity presented to us; making it important for us to learn how to tell ourselves, "No, not right now".

When we seek to accomplish greatness, and perform for accolades on the world's stage; we soon discover that our challenges will *always* be more significant than what we can handle on our own. If we seek to manage them on our own without God, we will never experience true victory. Consider those in the public eye—celebrities and politicians; no matter how much they accomplish for humanity, their adversities increase in volume. Don't ever forget that, "To he whom much is given, much is required." (Lk. 12:48) I am very humbled by that. I know that I could by no means tackle the issues of my church pastor, Oprah, or President Obama. I could not operate in that capacity....*I have not reached that diameter*!

As long as we continue to fight to maintain control over our journey and seek to defeat the enemy in our own strength, we will be like horses beating against the wind. Yet, God calls us to lay down our agendas and accept the fact that the problems in our society will always be greater than our individual capacity to resolve. He is looking for us to step back and allow Him to control every aspect. The choices we make and the relationships we manage— this is absolutely *His space* to reign. Here is the only place God will get the glory He deserves. And in return for glory, He will bless our lives with blessings beyond our wildest dreams. Like Jabez, He will enlarge our territories.

Here is the ultimate reward for enduring all of your hardships: as your problems increase –you increase. As the temperature of the fire increases, your prayers become more fervent. As the giants you encounter multiply in number and size, your faith to stand courageously will be tested. Undoubtedly, your confidence will increase as you withstand. The Apostle Paul stated: "*For I reckon that the sufferings of this present time are not worthy to be compared with the glory which shall be revealed in us.*" (Rom. 8:18) That's also why David said, "*It is good for me that I have been afflicted*" (Psalm 119:71). The more we allow God to have control of our lives, the greater our confidence, and the more opportunities we are presented for victory. The more giants I defeat, the more valuable I become!

I'm sure you will agree that the greater our problems tend to advance, the weaker we appear. As the mounts grow larger, we appear smaller. But I've learned, that the more frequently I endure and stand firm in the center of my storms, the more optimistic I become when faced with new storms. And that optimism grows only because of God's grace. See, when I can't find my way out of the darkness, and I feel trapped in a corner with no power, His grace is all I have.

> *And it shall come to pass, while My glory passeth by, that I will put thee in a cleft in the rock, and I will cover thee with My hand while I pass by;*
> *Exodus 33:22 KJV*

Each time that grace proves to be more than enough to carry me through. Paul tells us, "His strength is made perfect in my weakness." (2 Cor.12:9)

Some people mistakenly believe that to surrender is a sign of weakness. But Paul is saying just the opposite, "I just let Christ take over. And as a result, the more I surrender, the stronger I become".

Still, many times people ask the question "W*hy me God?* What did I do to deserve such a struggle? Why do I always seem to be fighting upstream, uphill, and against the wind?" I will admit that used to be my favorite chorus as well. But finally, one day, God asked me in response "*Why not you*?" And I thought to myself, "Okay how clever of Him." Soon I realized that as long as I have breath in my body, God will bless me.

I began to picture myself as that red colored clay on the potter's wheel. Think about it; the clay remains on the wheel, continually being pressed until the potter sees the finished product he originally had in mind. So, now as I faced my struggles, I echo the question, "*Why not me?*"

[5]*"Character is best formed in
the stormy billows of the world."*
Johann von Goethe

Do you believe that being hard-pressed produces character and maturity? Even though it's not an easy or comfortable experience for any of us, the pressing is a prerequisite for evolving into the beautiful creation God has in mind for you.

It is the pressing of the clay that brings it to its beautiful, undeniable 'character'. In Greek, character (*charakter*) is translated as 'image'. So, just as the Potter is pressing the clay to form the image He has created in His heart and mind, God is pressing us to form the image He originally intended for us, *His image*. That makes the pressing all worthwhile.

---

[5] Johann von Goethe c. – "Character is best formed in the stormy billows of the world."

During my seasons of great pain, I am always comforted once I understand the purpose of my pressure. I know that as long as I am being pressed, then God is not finished. Even when I thought I had become 'all that', I realized I had still not evolved into God's best version of me; God has something 'even better' in store! At that very moment, all I can say is, "WOW GOD"!

Now, people who know me personally have looked at my life and have often wondered, "How in the world do you keep surviving storm after storm? How do you find the strength to keep getting back up? Don't you get tired?" But all I can say is this, "I continue to stand strong in the midst of my storms; I recognize that if I am still alive to tell the story, then that means God still sees a greater glory to be revealed *in me*." In other words, I'm still standing because God still sees me as *fit for His use.*

We must also understand that if we have survived our tragedies, that God still sees a missing part of His image in us. God has begun a good work in each of us –and He intends to complete it. He won't leave any of His work *half-done.* So, let's put it like this: God wouldn't finish a project, leaving parts out, and settle for just a passing grade. He goes for a perfect score and bonus points! He pursues the "exceedingly and abundantly above all we could imagine!" (Eph.3:20)

At some point, we all have thought we were *'all that and a bag of chips'* and had *'arrived'.* Yet, our loving Father shows up again with His hands open wide, ready to *press again*. It catches me off guard and hurts quite a bit at first. The pressures of life begin, and I find myself broken down in disappointment or despair. But then I recognize that the beauty I thought I saw –was *nothing* compared to the beauty God sees. At this very moment, He is working to impress His image and instill right-living within me.

Furthermore, as He begins again with His pressing and molding, I hear God saying, "Kimberly there's more to you than meets *your* eye. You only see *part* of the finished masterpiece. Now let's get back to work."

When clay is confined to pressing by the potter's hands for long periods of time, the character produced in that vessel is not able to be duplicated. Perhaps, if a machine did it in computerized mass production, it can be imitated. But the original work done by the potter's hand can never be reproduced. There will always be a defining mark somewhere on the vessel that signifies that it is unique. There will only be one original. And likewise, we are all one of a kind!

I tend to stand taller when I consider that the amount of pressure and storms I've experienced will only produce one uncomparable, irreplaceable *Kimberly Michelle Ford*. Furthermore, I'm comfortable with admitting that my self-esteem increases every time I consider the fact that God created only one me. And, believe it or not, I am still being formed day by day. I don't have to envy another woman's gifts, looks, money, or wardrobe. My confidence grows by knowing that there is *only one* perfected me.

There is another noteworthy fact about the 'pressing that builds character'. And it is this: moments of extreme pressure are the only times you will witness authentic character. Genuine character is always demonstrated in the first reaction of an individual *under pressure*. Anyone can maintain their composure, smile, laugh, treat people nice, be honest, and make charitable contributions when they are in their comfort zone. Pretentious pastors and church leaders always tend to fall from grace during hard times. Sometimes, college graduates will commit crimes and then try to conceal their guilt. Naturally, when questioned they will admit they were under a lot of *pressure*. The church title may provide you with stature, and the college degree can provide you with wisdom. But you can only develop the character and image of God by being tested in the fire under pressure.

For in the time of trouble He shall hide me in His pavilion: in the secret of His tabernacle shall He hide me; He shall set me up upon a rock.
(Psalm27:5 NIV)

Scientists suggest that as one moves deeper into the center of the earth –the temperature and pressure experienced increases. Hmmm! Think about that! Let's apply that same principle to you and I. The closer you get to discovering your purpose (which is on the inside of you)

and identifying with the original image in which you were created, then the fire in your trials get hotter and the pressure you are forced to withstand intensifies. This progression doesn't surprise me; especially since Satan's most popular trick is to manipulate you out of your identity. The more you pursue authenticity, the challenge to stay the course will intensify. The enemy wants to discourage you. He wants you to become weary, overwhelmed with fear, and quit! He cannot risk you discovering your real identity. He fears that when you ascertain who *you are*, then you will be able to empower others to discover who *they are*!

Truth has a very distinct sound, and it horrifies the enemy. In my first book, "The Core", I discussed that when you make the decision to drive inward towards your core, and you begin to speak the truth—the enemy recognizes that sound. That boldness in your voice signifies the cry of battle. So, he immediately alerts every agent of darkness assigned to your life to take up their post. They are trained and ready to fight you every step of the way. It may be financial distress, by way of losing your job. The agent might show up in the form of extramarital affairs. The agent may also show up in the form of cancer, HIV, or some deadly virus.

But do not be afraid, in all of these attempts to knock you off balance. God will take you to a secret place, and He will hide you in it. If you allow Him, He will cover you and protect you. You won't run out of food; you won't wind up homeless, you won't contract the disease (and even if you do, how you respond to the condition is still a part of your assignment). No matter who left you, no matter who neglected you –you are never alone. You have "Yahweh Shammah" (meaning *The Lord is here*) right there in your corner. He will wrap you in His arms and comfort you in the fullness of His love. When you begin to rest in that, then no matter what he/she does to you, you can see them through God's eyes. You may be divorced from your spouse, and he/she may have abandoned your family. But while you are safely resting in God's arms, you can continue to love them as a brother/sister and pray for them to find Christ.

It is never easy to face our trials when we consider that those we love may get hurt along the way. But I am sure that if you take them with you into the presence of God, He will keep all of you in the protection of His arms. Trust Him to handle you and those you love. Even though God's arms are responsible for the painful pressing in my life, they are also accountable for comforting me in the process.

God knows just how much you can endure. He knows just how much you can bear. And God promises, like a careful potter, He'll bend you –and He may have to break you—but never beyond His ability to repair. He has created a sign that says, "Fragile Handle with Love" –and He's got more of that than you could ever imagine.

After all, it is His love that presses us, corrects us, keeps us, and heals us. Without that, the pressing would be meaningless. Without God's love, the pressing leaves us confused, drained, and depleted. Even in the darkest and worst of situations, I am comforted in knowing that I can withstand *it all* because He loves me. He'll never let me slip; He'll never let me fall –but He will always keep me centered in Him.

So, when you look around the corner, and you see darkness on the horizon, don't entertain fear and resentment. Instead, arise with the unexplainable peace of knowing that even the darkness is his love that you see. Catch your breath, square your shoulders, and prepare to go in the direction he sends you. Your confidence comes in knowing that he is your flashlight and your compass. Just follow his lead through the darkness and onto green pastures.

Can you imagine being "satisfied" *in the midst of famine*? Our heavenly father will surely provide everything you need for the journey. The moment you realize you have a need, provision will appear. You will learn to trust god as he gives you what you need –when you need it. You will discover that you always have more than enough.

As you travel the journey through this life, you will experience adversity. You might even have an encounter with the shadow of death. But, you will hear His voice drawing you; as you make your way through the thistles and the thorns. Our God is omnipotent. Even though He is up ahead compelling you to keep going, He is also right by your side. God didn't leave you to travel alone. As those who were sent to make the road rough for you laugh and prepare to celebrate your inevitable demise, He is preparing a feast for you to enjoy in their presence –at the finish. So, relax. He has carefully arranged of all the details. When your critics behold your victory table, even they will have to declare that the presence of the Lord is with you.

All of God's pressing will produce oil that keeps your mind moisturized, and furthermore drenched with His love. Your thinking will be clear, and bitterness won't have a hold on you. The beauty of God and His love for you will be on your heels all the way through. So, smile. Let the sun kiss your face and embrace the wind blowing across your head. Stand and behold the house where you can settle all of your anxieties…lay down your worries and your fears. You have a right to remain in *The House of the Lord*…forever.

Surely goodness and mercy shall follow me all the days of my
life and I will dwell in the house of the Lord Forever.
(Psalm 23:6 NKJV)

We are perplexed,
but not in despair...
(2Corinthians 4:9)

We're not sure what to do, but we
know that God knows what to do
(The Message)

3

JOY OVER DESPAIR

*W*hen a woman discovers that she is with child, in the early stages of development the fetus has no actual body formed. Have you ever marveled at the fact that even without a heart, the doctors are capable of performing an ultrasound and locating a heartbeat? I often imagine just how small the heart must be in that stage —maybe the size of a mustard seed?

God in His infinite wisdom and creative genius created us in such a way that the full lifecycle and successful development of humanity would be dependent upon that one small organ. Before God developed any of our other vital organs, He gave us a heart: *His heart.* Before God formed Adam and breathed life into him (Gen 2:7), what would become Adam's heart was already beating in the Father. Also, since Adam was the first to be born outside of a woman's womb, it is clear that it was the divine heart of God that beat first.

See, He formed man out of the clay. Then while breathing life into his nostrils, God transferred His heartbeat into Adam's heart. Moreover, at his heart's first contraction he immediately developed a pulse. Adam took his first breath and finally became a living being. So, it is this heartbeat, transferred by God alone, that still runs through all of humanity today.

Isn't it amazing when you consider the fact that no matter how many religions we have developed, no matter how many gods are being idolized and worshiped upon this earth, all of creation began with one single heartbeat? No matter how far off course from our Creator we have traveled, no matter how many wars we find a way to finance, we all continue to exist because of that one steady *heartbeat*.

At the time God made Earth and Heaven, before and grasses or shrubs had sprouted from the ground –God hadn't yet sent rain on Earth, nor was there anyone around to work the ground (the whole Earth was watered by underground springs) –God formed Man out of dirt from the ground and blew into his nostrils the breath of life. The Man came alive –a living Soul!

(Genesis 2:7 The Message Bible)

The fact that God gives us a heartbeat first, also tells us that the heart would need more time than every other part of the body to become fully developed. The strength of the human heart amazes me. It has a critical responsibility. However, in spite of its principal task—in my opinion, it is the most fragile part of our bodies. Our heart has the unique responsibility of pumping life into every organ in our body. Without it, every other organ in our bodies will immediately cease its function. Furthermore, humanity can pursue nothing apart from God's heartbeat and expect lasting success.

We have all experienced the effect of having our own pity party. Sometimes we have them alone. Sometimes we have guests to join us. Have you ever been so deep in despair that you actually discover the bottom of your pit? Depression is not a bottomless pit. There really is a floor. Those of you who have traveled to this place in your life, know that even though you will never find it on a map, you can attest to the fact that it does exist. You can relate to the phrase *rock bottom* and how *rock bottom* actually feels. Because of the pain associated with *rock bottom*, all of you would agree you would never 'choose' to go there and don't ever want to go there again. Then there are some like me, who have been hard-headed and driven themselves back to rock bottom more than once.

During one of my trips to rock bottom, I realized that it was in these dark moments that I could actually *feel* the healing power of my Father. On this trip, I endured the heartache of a pending divorce. At first, of course, I'd use different things like music, movies, and overloading myself with work to numb the pain and drown out the thoughts racing in my mind. My thoughts would vascillate between ideas about *who did what* and *what we could have done differently*. Suddenly, once God managed to get me alone, I could literally feel Him wrap His loving arms around me. As I lie in my bed awake at night—broken, afraid, and struggling to make sense of it all –His embrace would calm my soul.

Looking back over the years, I can admit that there were times when I felt like God had let me down. No matter how much I prayed, fasted, and drenched my husband and our house down in oil…my family still fell apart. Most nights in my husband's absence, I'd be up all-night praying. I'd go throughout the house anointing the walls with holy oil. I'd rub the doorknobs in oil. I'd drip oil in each of his shoes. I'd drip oil from the doorstep, then down the walkway; down the driveway all the way to the end of the property line at the street. I'd rub his pillow, the shower head, the towels, sinks, and even drop oil in the very rugs where he would stand: beside the bed and in the bathroom in front of the sink. Several nights after he had come home drunk and fell on the sofa instead of coming to bed I'd go in the living room and drop olive oil in his hair, in his shoes and even on his Blackberry. I left no spot uncovered.

I did all this with the hopes of warding off the "contaminated thoughts" that were controlling him and drove him to drink and wander the streets at night. I firmly believed that it would only be by the blood of Jesus that he'd be covered and protected from the traps of sin. I knew that he was lost and just needed to find his own way to

God. But, I figured I could at least keep him covered until he saw the light.

I laid there on my bedroom floor morning after morning and night after night; pleading, begging, and believing God for a change in my marriage. However, I kept feeling there was something I was doing wrong. It appeared God just refused to grant me this one wish. I'd leap for every little light of hope that would come from my husband, suggesting that he might be at the door of a breakthrough. Still, the late nights and overnight tears would fall, as I wondered "Where is my husband"? Why can't he come home? I often thought, "Doesn't God hear me down here? Can't He see the tears and my sweat in my hands?" I knew God loved me, I've known Him all my life. But according to this one request…God wouldn't seem to budge.

> *Love never stops loving. It extends beyond the gift of prophecy, which eventually fades away. It is more enduring than tongues, which will one day fall silent. Love remains long after words of knowledge are forgotten.*
>
> *(1 Corinthians 13:8 TPT)*

Three months after my husband had abandoned us, I finally felt God wiping the tears from my eyes. When he first left, I refused to cry. He had threatened to abandon us so many times, and I'd already cried so many tears. I was quite ready to move on and live. I refused myself the luxury of feeling the pain of rejection and abandonment. I couldn't let the kids see me broken down again. So, by keeping myself busy with work and the kids, I avoided the tears.

Perplexed about *how* and *why* he could walk away from us, his family, without looking back –I wound up reaching out for drinks at the bar. Because of my disappointment, I began to rebel by reaching for the things I had overcome and rose above (the club scene, alcohol, sex, bitter music). I started longing for the touch of another human being. But really, I just wanted the pain of abandonment to go away. "Why try? Why pray?" I thought. Most saints won't admit that they entertain these thoughts. Still, I found myself entertaining bitter thoughts and feelings about how God ignored my prayer requests and allowed this to happen. I even allowed myself to consider for a short while that God wasn't faithful to His promises.

After the alcohol would wear off, and I made it home from the bar in one piece, I soon realized that what I ultimately desired was *God's love*. Once again, I felt I was in the absence of love. Paul tells us in 1 Corinthians 13:8 that "Love never fails." However, during this season, I began to entertain the idea and imagined that *God's unconditional love* had failed me.

I thought no matter what my ex-husband did, as long as I forgave him in my heart and did my best to forget what happened, then he would always return with his vow "to have and to hold," through the good and the bad.

The vow was golden between us in the beginning. Now it seemed to never be enough to get us through the arguments. The more I forgave, the more I felt *abandoned*. The more mercy I showed, the more I felt *mocked* for my faith in God's ability to restore us. Even though I loved the Lord enough to love my husband—beyond his human faults, I began to feel *punished*. Why? It appeared that God would not answer my prayers and heal our marriage. But I knew that was not God's likeness. Abandoned, mocked, punished—these are all emotions crafted by the enemy himself to cause us to deny God. On the contrary, God honors all of the sacrifices we make for Him.

Then it happened. One night, this Friday night, on my way home from work, I couldn't stop the tears from falling. I finally felt the hand of my Father wiping the tears from my eyes. I began to wonder, "Why now God? Where were you when I was praying, fasting, and believing in a change?" Why could He answer these tears, but not all the others?

In that divorce, I learned that some people could give us the best of themselves that they have to offer. Still, it may not be God's best for us. Clearly, my Father had another plan for my life.

Now, God is here to heal. He knew the days that lay ahead of me. The Lord also knew about the day we would face the result of our decision in divorce court. He comforted me during that day in the courtroom. It became clear to me that just as He was with me in the thick of the turmoil, He's also with me right now. *He kept me* because

I prayed. *He kept me* because I fasted. *He kept me* because I anointed my husband and my home. *He kept me* because I gave Him my sweat and my tears!

When my husband first left, I felt incredibly cheated. It wasn't supposed to end this way, *I thought*. I was supposed to pray, and He was supposed to stay...until things changed. We were supposed to grow old and watch our children grow together. He was supposed to be my prince charming and grant me my happily ever after...*I thought*. Didn't I say I was praying for change? Yes! Things surely changed.

Since God *sustained me* in my season of distress, I can recognize that it wasn't my ex-husband who had changed; but it was me who in fact had drawn closer and closer to God. Moreover, when God began to shift me closer towards my destiny, he simply was not prepared to shift with me. Though shifting synchroniously is not required, it may make one party very uncomfortable. The reflection of who I was becoming in my relationship with God, forced my spouse to examine himself and acknowledge where he fell short in his own. This left him with an important decision to make: remain in the marriage and grow closer to God or abandon our relationship. Though we divorced, I continue to pray for his salvation.

However, thanks to that experience, and the times I spent worrying about my marriage, I grew stronger and wiser. I know it was only because of my sincere desire to understand why things were going in the wrong direction for us, that I called on Jesus louder and louder. As the days, months, and years went by, each obstacle we faced in our marriage drove me straight to my knees. Each situation inspired me to find a mirror to look within Kimberly to find out what I contributed to the problem. I yearned for my marriage to work and I always wanted to choose a mature reaction to his actions. I didn't always do things correctly. I was very young, so at times I said things at the wrong time. However, I earnestly desired to bring the ultimate result, *reconciliation.*

I constantly asked myself did I really have the love of Christ flowing through my veins? Could I really love like He loved and forgive in the same manner that He forgives? Well, loving and living with someone who does not share the same belief system will surely test your ability to love as Christ loves.

God began to reveal to me that anytime I felt void of the unconditional love I so desperately sought, it was right then (at that very moment) that *He* wanted to love me. Wow! Talk about a shocking discovery! I was learning that the unconditional love that I expected from my spouse could only come from one place...my Father. My Father did something so great for me in that marriage. Moreover, because of the rejection I experienced, I understand God's love for me more *now*, than I ever did before. He was wise enough to secure the power of that love right down inside of me. And it flows! Oh yes! It flows like a river from within me.

It is easy to love those who love you back and forgive those who are truly remorseful. It's never easy to love the unlovable or forgive the unforgiveable. However, I learned in this relationship that it can be done –if you desire reconciliation intensely enough. As we attempt to move forward, and love those who have hurt us, we may become hindered in our efforts by wondering "why, how, and what if." In the end, it's all about the power of God's love, not ours.

We have to remember that God does not promote the confusion of "*why, how, and what if.*" Otherwise, He will always promote the development of our confidence in Him – because He knows what He is doing. I mean *what if* He had to ask Himself the same questions when He selected humankind to reflect His image in the earth? He could have easily hovered above the earth and questioned, "What if they fail?' What if they deny me? What if they don't love me in return?"

However, He could project victory beyond all our foreseen faults; even though He knew we would *indeed* fail along the way. He knew we would periodically forget His sovereign power, become frustrated, throw in the towel, and quit. He was well aware that we would periodically forget His omniscience and begin to worry. Still, He pressed on – and *formed* us anyhow. It's like God knew He was making a "mess" (because sometimes we have to admit that we are a mess!), but He made it anyhow!

Let me let you in on a little secret, and I know this is going to sound so cliché. Since we were chosen to be representatives of His image –we look like Him. So Yes! Since God, our Father, is the Creator of pressing on – we are designed to *press on (in Him)*. He looked beyond what He knew we would do and pressed on to create an incomparable glory. So, if He could push beyond the inevitable obstacles of why, how, and what if, don't you think you have the same power within you to advance beyond your own uncertainty?

First, let's deal with *why*. To ask *why* is to ask: "for what cause, reason, or purpose." That has become my first quiz. Instead of allowing my *why* to be an object of confusion, I will turn it around and use it to increase my wisdom. I don't just ask why. Instead, I ask, "What is the cause and purpose of my storm." Do you see how I took one word and inverted the meaning of it? Instead of asking "Why" from a position of feeling despair and forsaken, now the "Why" becomes the caveat for opportunity and breakthrough. Now I am not necessarily focused on the negative aspect of my storm. I am focused on the reward God intends for me to receive as a result of the storm. Once we learn this, then we can use our adversity to bring Him the ultimate glory.

The best way to confront each storm is first to acknowledge that God 'causes' each storm to form. Then remember, scientifically speaking, each *cause* must have an *effect*. So, the next question is: What impact will you allow this storm to have in your life? Will you let it affect your prayer life in a way that you draw near unto God? Will the effect in your life be a greater passion for charity, giving, and outreach? Alternatively, will the effect of your storm be a loss of faith, weight loss/gain, depression, or suicidal ideations?

When I embrace the fact that it was God's *cause* that formed the storm, then I can embrace my responsibility to determine the effect. That is a valuable lesson to learn. Though God forms the storm for His very own *cause*, He gave us full *autonomy* to determine the *impact*. God seeks a precise result. So, until the storm serves its original purpose, the storm will be forced to begin over and over again.

Usually, in times of extreme pressure, we immediately cry out, "Oh it hurts!" or "Why me?" It is critical that we develop the courage to drive into the darkness (to identify the real purpose of the storm) and declare that we will not allow it to have an adverse effect, but one that brings glory to God. Then (and only then) we will begin to transform into whom God intended for us to be. As a result, *that* particular storm can come to an end.

Real peace begins in the middle of the storm. One of my favorite psalmists, Yolanda Adams, sang it best when she sang: "Jesus *kept me* in the midst of the storm!" The authenticity of peace does not even begin to exist –until tested in the storm!

Whenever I decide to take it upon myself to ask *why* I am in a particular situation, I turn around like my Father would have done and ask myself, "Why not?" If I ask, "God why did he leave me here alone to struggle with three kids?" God says, "Why not?" "Why did I lose my job during a recession?" God asks, "Why not?" "Why do I feel so abandoned and rejected?" Again, He asks, "Kimberly, Why not?" I can now understand His *why not* – because I know if He brought me to this place in my life, He apparently has a purpose and a plan for it.

The next question we have a habit of singing like a middle school chorus on repeat is *how*?

- *How* did this tragedy happen?
- *How* did I get here?
- *How* will I overcome?
- *How* will I make it?
- *How* will I survive?

The list goes on. We can remain suspended in time searching for an escape from what may appear to be our demise. We can hover over our bills wondering *how* we will find the resources to assist us with the down payment on a home. We can stare up the corporate ladder trying to figure out *how* we will ever reach the top. We can sit on the sides of our beds and gaze into the future and wonder *how* we can reposition our lives in a place of fulfillment and off of the hopeless path we appear to be traveling. The truth is, asking *how* never got *me* any results.

Leave your impoverished confusion and live! Walk up the street to a life with meaning"

(Proverbs 9:1 The Message Bible)

Generally, we don't receive clear results by anxiously twiddling our thumbs and expecting an answer to appear like a light bulb. But I am convinced, that the creative power to change any situation is within me. To ask *how* is to ask, "in what manner?" We've done it again! We have inverted the word *how* which previously had us conditioned with fear and doubt. Now, the word *how* positions us to consider the numerous possibilities by which God could manifest His blessings. In what manner will my help come? In what way will my bills be paid? In what manner will my marriage be saved? In what manner will my child be delivered? In what manner will my body be healed?

Here is a bonus. When we invert *the question 'how'*, we not only position ourselves to consider all the possibilities. We also reposition ourselves from doubt to expectation. Talk about taking a word and turning it upside down!

Most times, we resort to asking *how* because we don't think that there is an answer. If we look at it the wrong way, asking *how* can create the perception that we are trapped or cornered without options. Well, after several opportunities to test God's word, I've discovered that He has already provided a solution to every problem we will ever encounter. He has already offered a way of escape. Would you consider for a moment that when He created *you*–He also created every single one of your escape plans? As a reminder, the details concerning your life were finalized before He even *formed* you.

God has already given us options. Unfortunately, we will not identify those options as we stagger through life on the paradigm of anxiety and frustration.

Why should I sway in anxiety when I know that my Father already has a solution worked out for me? Why run in circles, call every friend crying, or lie in my bed worrying when I have been empowered to get up out of my bed and take a drive down the highway to be refreshed and find peace? Why waste time worrying about *how*, when the only way I will find resolve is by trusting my Father enough to place the burden exclusively in His hands?

The great psalmist, Louisa M.R. Stead, wrote:

[6]*'Tis so sweet to trust in Jesus,*
Just to take Him at His Word;
Just to rest upon His promise,
And to know, "Thus saith the Lord!

It is indeed so sweet to trust in Jesus and to take Him at his word! Life is so much sweeter when we learn to let Jesus take the wheel and get out of the driver's seat. When you were a kid and first got your driver's license you were so excited to drive. You would probably even drive to the mailbox to get the mail. Over time, the more you drove

---

[6] *Louisa M.R. Stead c. 1850-1917–" 'Tis so sweet to trust in Jesus,…"*

and the older you got, you discovered that driving was indeed work and not fun at all. Aren't you tired of driving? Move over to the passenger seat, hit the recline switch, and enjoy the ride!

Jesus gave us the right to come to Him with our burdens and cast them upon His shoulders. Then, He promised if we did that—He would give us rest. Oh, that word sounds like music to my ears every time I hear it. *Rest!* Oh, just imagine what it feels like to get over your dilemma and simply rest! Give God the financial burden; take a drive to the country, and *rest!* Give Jesus the doctor's report and *rest!*

If we sat in fear and never matured beyond our apprehension, it would be because we were entertaining our old friend *what if? What if* I have AIDS? *What if* I lose my job? *What if* I fail? *What if* I don't get healed? *What if* my kids get hurt? *What if* my spouse leaves me? What if we lose our home?

What you are really asking in all of this is: "What if God doesn't show up?" Can you imagine that? *God actually not showing up?* I can't. So why even consider it? Why even entertain negative thoughts and ideas that would suggest we serve a God that does not show up? He is not created like man; therefore, He does not have the ability to lie.

Many times, we take things into our own hands out of fear; not just rebellion or disobedience. We assume control because we are secretly afraid that His word may not work in this or that situation. We tend to think that because we cannot see Him, then He is not present. We sometimes believe He just may be a little too busy with war and world hunger to be concerned about "little me." Well newsflash: God does not respect any one person or group over the other. He is just as concerned about you and your three kids as He is about the entire country of Africa.

The best remedy for the old "what if" disease is a good dose of speaking of those things that you *want* to happen –as though they *already happened.* If you desire to buy a home for your family, whether you have the money for the down payment or not, make a habit of saying, "We are moving soon!" If you are divorced, and you truly desire to be married, then you need to start your sentences with, "When I get married again…" Be careful not to say "IF." The word *IF* only supports your doubt and presents that you have a percentage of disbelief.

If you are facing a dilemma and you're afraid of the appearance of a traumatic outcome, remember that the victory lies in the words you speak. Whatever you call it, is what it will be. If you call it divorce, it will be divorce. If you name it layoff/job loss, then the outcome will be a pink slip. If you call out sickness, what you will feel is disease.

Another remedy for the negative what-if's is to invert those negative what-if's into positive ones. Take every negative idea and replace it with a positive outlook. Altering your perspective this way will re-train your mind to think optimistically about your future. Many people attempt to protect themselves from disappointment by labeling themselves 'realists.' Still, given the condition of our economy and our political climate, everybody can benefit from a big dose of optimism.

Here's an example:

Negative	Positive
What if I die from AIDS?	*What if* I lead others to Christ by my faith for healing?
What if I lose my job?	*What if* I am selected for promotion on my job?
What if I fail?	*What if* I make history by being the first to succeed?
What if my spouse abandons me?	*What if* God heals my marriage?
What if God doesn't show up?	*What if* God performs a miracle in my life?

A simple definition of perplexity is: *a dis-ease of the mind (a mind not at ease)* We all know what it feels like for our minds to not be *at ease*. Sometimes things that should come naturally can prove to be our highest area of challenge. Sometimes we develop ways to become comfortable in chaos and settle for a life filled with confusion in an attempt to avoid facing the challenge of *change*.

We'd rather do nothing—than to get up, activate our faith, and trust in Him.

Contrarily, I've found that it is so much easier to re-member all God requires is that I trust Him. If I relied on my own faulty thinking, the circumstances in my life would be a complete mess. I would have never developed the courage and self-love to overcome the heartache and unexplainable rejection I have experienced. Therefore, I promise you the key to your freedom is all in your *release*. *Release* the confusion. *Release* the anxiety. *Release* the problem from your hand and turn it over to Him.

The moment we realize we are not able to resolve a problem, that is the moment we should embrace the fact that the problem belongs to Him. The longer we exert all our efforts and our strength on conflict that belongs to God, the more damage we do to our own health.

Do you think your Father who loves you, wants you worried, confused, and stressed out over a problem He never intended for you to solve on your own? He invited you to present your requests to Him. So yes—take them to *Him*. Not your mother, your girlfriend, or your spouse. Let *Him* know what you want Him to resolve. Let *Him* know you trust *Him* enough to resolve it. Thank *Him* in advance for the finished work. Then, show *Him* you mean business by leaving it there. Don't pick it back up. Don't carry it away from your posture of prayer. Also, I can promise you that if you do like He says, He will grant you with wisdom… *liberally* (that is generously, abundantly, and freely).

I am thoroughly convinced my Father has given us more wisdom than we could ever fathom. The saying goes that "If you take one step towards Him, He'll take two towards you." So, if we just tell Him and show Him that we trust Him to handle the crisis (however He pleases), we will discover indescribable peace. If you want to be confused about anything, let it be about how you found *peace* in the midst of your confusion.

Just think, if He could create the heavens and the earth and solve the complex problem of how to keep it all perfectly in place, then surely, He can do a much better job keeping your life intact. But only *if you trust Him*!

[7]*"Joy runs deeper than despair!" –Corrie ten Bloom*

One thing I know for sure about myself is that at first, on the surface you *may* see me a little anxious and confused about a situation. I don't consider myself to be perfect; we are all human. However, somewhere, way down deep inside of me –there is hope (an assurance) that all will end well. That hope helps me to reconnect with the love of my Father. Soon enough, that love will begin to resonate from within me. It permeates my soul to the extent that despair does not stand a chance up against it. My heart can rejoice and sing with gladness as if it never misses a beat. My joy comes in knowing that my Father is *here.* His presence grants me freedom from agonizing and worrying over something that is too big for me to handle.

---

[7] Corrie ten Bloome c. - "Joy runs deeper than despair!"

No matter what I experience. No matter who leaves, no matter what I *think* I lost, I can *rest*...knowing that the Father *is here*! I feel His heart beating. He *is* with me. Immanuel? Ahhhh! Yes! That's His name...*God with us.*

[8] "*When circumstances seem impossible, when all signs of grace in you seem at their lowest ebb, when temptation is fiercest, when love and joy and hope seem nigh extinguished in your heart, then rest, without feeling, and without emotion, in the Fathers faithfulness.*" *–David Tryon*

---

[8] *David Tryon c.* "*When circumstances seem impossible, when all signs of grace in you seem at their lowest ebb, when temptation is fiercest, when love and joy and hope seem nigh extinguished in your heart, then rest, without feeling, and without emotion, in the Fathers faithfulness.*" *–David Tryon*

We are persecuted,
but not in despair...
(2Corinthians 4:9)

We've been spiritually terrorized,
but God hasn't left our side
(The Message)

4

ENDURING PERSECUTION WITH GRACE

So, what did they say? What did you hear? How did it make you feel? Just what if you hadn't heard it? What if you had chosen not to listen? Would you really care? Many people will boast that they give no thought to what others think about them. Don't believe the lie. We were all created with the desire to be accepted and loved. Yet, some have the propensity to pretend they are non-chalant in an effort to safegaurd themselves from the pain of rejection.

Transparently, I have asked myself on many occasions, "What is it about the opinions and perceptions of others that drive me mad?" For most of my life, I have stood in the corner or somewhere in the background listening as others assassinated my character, persecuted me as I endured painful trials, and crucified me with the lashing of their tongues. Even more, for the first one-third of my life, almost every decision and move I made, was based off what somebody or some group of people said about me. Either, I had to prove somebody right, I had to prove somebody wrong, or I had to prove to myself that I was not crazy or a failure as people would have me to believe.

When I had a miscarriage at 15, *they whispered.* When I had my first abortion, they talked. When I danced in the strip clubs, they stared as *they talked.* When I gained a little weight, *they talked.* When I was being abused, they shook their heads, and *they talked.* When I decided to change my life and to follow Christ *they mocked,* and *they talked.* When I married a manager, co-workers *–they did talk.* When I accepted my call to ministry, in disbelief *–they talked.* When he had the affairs, *they talked.* When I bought the Mercedes, with jaws dropping *they talked.* When we separated and got divorced, they assumed, and *they continued to talk.*

> *"The heart is deceitful above all things, and desperately wicked; who can know it?"*
>
> *(Jer 17:9 NKJV)*

But as I have embarked upon the 2nd wind of my life, I've experienced an epiphany that screams loud and clear, "So what!" I have learned that no matter how much or how little "*they*" think they know, people will still talk. I have discovered that the people who have time to conjure up stories and entertain themselves with the events of my life, just have *nothing* better to do. Furthermore, many people have just never tamed the power of their own tongue.

"You have minds like a snake pit! How do you suppose what you say is worth anything when you are so foul-minded? It's your heart, not the dictionary, which gives meaning to your words. A good person produces good deeds and words season after season. An evil person is blight on the orchard. Let me tell you something: Every one of these careless words is going to come back to haunt you. There will be a time of Reckoning. Words are powerful; take them seriously. Words can be your salvation. Words can also be your damnation." (Matthew 12:34-37 The Message)

One of the smallest parts of the body, the tongue, has been known to start catastrophic wars among nations and do extreme irreversible damage. It has also been known to destroy families and cripple communications across generational lines. The things people say to or about each other can do one of two things: build them up in empowerment or tear them down in the offense. Typically, when somebody says something to hurt or offend another person, it is without realizing that he/she has offended anyone. It is unfortunate that you can be in a relationship with a friend or spouse for many years relying merely on their words, only to find out that all along you have been deceived about their true feelings.

We already know that the heart is very deceiving. So, if the words of our mouth reflect the meditation of our hearts, then we can be easily deceived even by those who are closest to us. They have also deluded themselves. Things that are spoken to us and over our lives by those who claim to "love" us can be easily miscommunicated and misinterpreted. For example, a man tells his wife, "I love you, and I simply cannot live without you." This is translated by the wife as unconditional affection. However, in the man's sub-conscience there lies the thought, "If she starts nagging me to do the things that make me uncomfortable (like asking him to pray as a couple) I am as good as gone."

> *In the multitude of words, sin is not lacking, but he that restrains his lips is wise*
> *(Proverbs 10:19NKJV)*

> *Whoever hides hatred hides lying lips, and whoever spreads slander is a fool.*
> *(Proverbs 10:18 NKJV)*

Here, is where it is essential to use your discernment (judgment) to discover what the unspoken truth really is. You may hear the words that come out of their mouths, but the question remains, what are they really saying? It's never easy to determine the truth in a person's heart, but it isn't rocket science either. Naturally, we want to believe the best and hope for the best in our relationships. Still, many times, unfortunately, we are forced to accept the worst when it happens. It's never painless to discover you have been betrayed and criticized by loved ones, or anyone for that matter. Some people may attempt to give us the perception that they are unbothered. This is a very dangerous coping mechanism, positioning the wounded for an emotional explosion somewhere down the road. Betrayal is a painful and discouraging experience. When you begin to pay enough attention to the work of the tongue (things people say) and line them up with the things they do (body language) you will learn to identify people who are authentic.

If an individual is *wise*, he/she will speak clearly and fluently on a subject matter. A wise person will also know when to speak and when it is crucial to be silent and listen. King Solomon quotes "*Wisdom is found on the lips of him who has understanding*" (*Proverbs 10:13*) Nehemiah knew to be silent until he was prepared to approach the king with his plans to rebuild the walls (Neh.2:16). He waited until he fully understood the situation and had counted the cost of the work to be done before he went running to the king with his proposal.

O generation of vipers, how can ye, being evil, speak good things? For out of the abundance of the heart the mouth speaketh.

(Matthew 12:34 NKJV)

Being wise with our words will also require self-control. It is much easier to succumb to the natural response of cursing someone out after they have unjustly criticized us. But to be considered wise, there are times when you must deny yourself the right to react. We gain influence and grow in stature with people when we can demonstrate our ability to resist 'foolishness.' James tells us "*If any of you lack wisdom, let him ask of God, who giveth to all men liberally and without reproach, and it shall be given to him. (James 1:5)*

If an individual has *integrity*, he/she won't entertain or tolerate gossip. When others lie and say things that destroy your character, it may appear that you and those who know you, may have been denied the unquestionable truth. To be quite honest, the truth *about* you lies *in you*, not in the opinions of others. There is an old saying that goes "a lie will spread much faster than the truth." Sometimes, the energy behind a lie is seemingly much more forceful than the truth. The reason for that is some people will more quickly believe and then repeat a lie *quicker* than they will believe and repeat the truth. One person hears it, repeats it, and it soon gains its momentum. Once the story lands upon its third and fourth set of ears, it has become the gospel. It has always amazed me how people will repeat things they have heard (simply because it makes "good conversation") without waiting for the facts to be revealed first. If some individual repeats what he or she has seen or heard, he becomes a partaker of the sinful act. Once something has been repeated, fact or fiction, all who repeat it are guilty of the same crime. Therefore, even Solomon declared spreading gossip as "the sport of a fool."

If an individual has developed *character*, he/she will instead cleverly redirect the gossiper's conversation to how he or she can use their criticism to create positive change. In the mouth of a person with mature character lies a 'controlled' tongue. When you begin to reject the opportunity to indulge in gossip, naysayers may mock you and consider you weak. But what's most important is that you are growing and developing character.

When we exist in our carnal nature, this breeds a life of drama and confusion. Contrarily, when we operate in our spiritual nature, taking a position of silence, we can place our focus on Christ and not ourselves. As a result, we gain understanding. God desires that we live a life of peace. He never promised us a life without experiencing persecution or rejection. Ratherm he has demonstrated a way for us to live in peace, even as we are being misunderstood.

People who are entertained by the sport of gossip are very easily influenced. Gossip run's rampant in our churches and places of employment. Whatever TMZ, CNN, and Good Morning America are laughing at today, our church family and co-workers are laughing too. If the news media reports an event as sad, then they are hopeless. If the media has judged and sentenced someone accused of a crime (before they have been rightly tried in court) then in their eyes as well –the person is perceived as guilty. Those who are not sensitive to the recovery process someone must endure when their character has been assassinated, have no clue as to how much damage is being done.

Dear reader, if you are the one suffering from this crime, I want to encourage you. Rest assured, the very same people who are laughing today –are the same people who will ultimately look up to you tomorrow. They will seek you out for advice. During their times of distress, they will refer back to you in awe and amazement. They will wonder how you made it through *your* storms.

For we all often stumble and fall and offend in many
things. And if anyone does not offend in speech [never says
the wrong things], he is a fully developed character and a per-
fect man, <u>able to control his whole body and to curb</u>
<u>his entire nature</u>.
(James 3:2 Amp)

Answer this: how can anybody understand the intricate details lining the fabric of your being –better than God himself? *Who* knows how far you can fly, how far you can go, or just how much you can bear –besides God? *Who* can see the molecules and atoms that come together to create your matter *besides God*? *Who* knows how much mass you consist of *besides God*? And *who* knows just how much space (territory) you are created to dominate –*besides God*?

Persecution also creates confusion within you. Before you may have felt like you were victorious. Then, after hearing the voices of friends and relatives speaking negatively about you, you may begin to feel like you need to go back and question what God spoke to you in the secret place with Him. We are affirmed and secured in our secret place, but now out here among unbelievers, it is easy to develop a great sense of insecurity and self-doubt.

Here is the resolve that may end your confusion: What God says *to us* and *about us* in our intimate moments with Him are the most authentic moments of our lives. What He declares is not to be questioned or confused with what others think or say about you.

Persecution has the capacity to convert your adversities and opportunities for growth into notable failures. It builds a wall of doubt that you will eventually be forced to do the work of tearing back down.

The aspect of persecution that we must remember is that this is not a mere physical battle, it is a spiritual battle. Verbal abuse is an act of the flesh that seeks to tear down every pillar of hope that abides within us. Persecution is also a stronghold designed to entrap us emotionally and then bind us up in rejection, neglect, and condemnation. When we are emotionally bound by verbal assaults, we are not capable of producing. We are not capable of carrying out the plan of God for our lives. At this point, we are distracted and spiritually paralyzed. When our prayer lives are not healthy, and we are not living a consecrated life, persecution will be successful to do just that—*tear us down.*

We know that we are spiritual beings, housed in earthen vessels, having an earthly experience. So how do we measure the dimensions of our being? We can't see our spirit with our natural eyes, so how can we recognize the things we are made of? Even moreso, how can we ever learn what we are truly capable of?

Like our enemies, we can look in the mirror and see the physical manifestation of God's hands. We are His creation. Yet with our natural eyes, we cannot see what resources we have on the inside. Still, you have an advantage that the enemy doesn't have. You (and only you) have a direct line of communication to God, through which He will reveal to you the dimensions of your spirit. Only He can show you the height, the depth, and the width of His power in you. There are testimonies of things that God has done *for* you and *in* you that only you and God know about.

> *And when they were come to the place which is called Calvary, there they crucified him and the malefactors one on the right hand and the other on the left. Then said Jesus, "Father forgive them for they know not what they do." And they parted his raiment and cast lots.*
> *(Luke 23:33-34 NKJV)*

Let's look at the scientific definitions of *matter, mass,* and *volume. Matter* is defined as anything that takes up space, can be perceived by our senses, and has mass. In our daily living, matter refers to the stuff. Ever had someone to ask, "What is *the matter* with you?" What they are really asking is, "What is your *issue*?" "What is the *stuff* you are dealing with?" They are not necessarily asking *how much stuff* are you dealing with or the magnitude of *it* in your life; they are simply asking what *"it"* is.

Mass is the amount of matter that forms a body and has some kind of shape and size. Now here is where people want to know how much stuff you are dealing with. Here is where you attempt to describe just how the stuff is really affecting your life. The amount of stuff (matter) you are dealing with reveals to others what you are worth (or mass).

There is a fine line between what you are dealing with and who you are. Because of this fine line, sometimes people mistakenly identify or label themselves as the stuff they are dealing with. Like if I have been raped, I will likely identify myself as 'the raped girl'; or if I have been mistreated as a child, I may mark myself as 'abused.' Though many may label you as your experience and call you by their names, it *is not* who you are. You are not defined by your experiences.

An object's 'weight' is used to determine how much matter or mass that object has. Now, you can look at those things (matters) that have weighed you down, and use them as leverage to elevate yourself. Think about this, the more matter you put on the scale, the weight increases. As it relates to you, my dear friend, the more obstacles you overcome, the more persecution you endure, the more stuff you are given to carry –your weight increases, the sturdier and more robust you become. When God puts you and someone who has not experienced as much on the scale, your side of the scale inevitably tips over and you are comparingly "worth more in weight" than the person hanging on the opposing side.

Volume is defined merely as "the amount of space that matter takes up." Volume suggests the size of the territory that you are destined to occupy and reign in. Volume defines the space that you are given dominion over.

Only God knows how much warfare you are equipped to handle. When I think of the word volume, it reminds me of my mountains; our mountains reflect the '*matter*', and the size of the mountain reflects their '*volume*'. To sum up the whole point here: The mountain is the matter that has mass and takes up space (space which is volume).The situation is your mountain –and the volume tells us how severe it is.

If I look at the mountains I have had to climb in life, I realize that the bigger the mountain became, the greater the volume increased. As mountains (matter) become more substantial in size, their base grows wider (volume). For example, let's just say you need to pay a phone bill and don't have the money. To most individuals, that is considered a 'small mountain'. It does not affect your sleep, eating, or your emotions. Now, on the other hand, let's say that your doctor reports to you that the migraines are being caused by a tumor lodged in an inoperable position in your brain. This is undoubtedly a much large mountain which a much larger base!

This becomes even more difficult when you combine limited finances and insufficient medical insurance. I am sure you can attest to the fact that the most significant times of adversity in your life, required more strength for you to keep moving forward. Bigger mountains drain our energy, arrest our focus, and consume more of our prayers. When we stare back at the overwhelming mountains in front of us, instead of joy and sweet peace, anguish and fear become our bedtime buddies. The bigger the mountain, the more strategic and resilient you must be in your efforts to make it to the other side.

Many people agree that perception is the reality. Persecution comes in many forms. Most times it's in the form of lies and delusion. For example, the enemy would have me to believe that I am defeated. I am convinced that is a lie.

There is a rule that we should all live by, and it says simply, "*Garbage in—Garbage out.*" This means whatever garbage enters your ears by way of gossip, slander, and persecution—throw it out quickly with yesterday's trash! Don't hold on to it. Don't meditate on it. The more you practice this principle you will soon discover that it becomes more effective to ignore or end the conversation, disregarding what you have heard.

I had to learn at a very early age that everybody in our lives will not be happy with our growth and success. Usually, we are surprised and disappointed when we learn that the unhappy campers may be those very close to us. Hiding their secret envy, these very people will look for ways to discredit or water down your testimony. You may hear rumors like you cheated on the exams. Some will say you took a shortcut to get where you are financially. Or, they will suggest you compromised your integrity to get a promotion. We absolutely must not allow the allegations of those who are obviously green with envy to cause us to abort God's plans for our lives.

Maybe your name has been publicly scrutinized before the world at large. It's not just your family, friends in school, or co-workers who look at you in shame; but we are talking about the entire human race. Maybe you have been accused of sexual abuse in the presence of the whole Christian community. That is a huge mountain to climb.

Well, that's exactly what happened to a very prominent pastor. The entire scandal, driven by tabloids and a media-savvy lawyer seeking fame, caused the integrity of the pastor and the entire church family to endure a public trial. As the church family unified in vigorous prayer and support for their leader, many criticized by saying they were a brainwashed cult. The church family had endured persecution from naysayers, the media, and government before; but this was the mountain of all mountains.

Now, for a man who has dedicated his life to developing young men without fathers –so they would become strong, productive, and honorable men –this accusation proved to be the most massive mountain he'd ever encounter. It was at the very heart of the pastor to see single mothers have acces to an abundant and prosperous life. He demonstrated his compassion by providing food, homes, cars, and financial aid regularly. On many occasions, he lent himself as a foster parent –willing to stand in the gap and assume the spiritual responsibility of a father –seeking to fill the deep void in their hearts created by the absent men in their lives.

Many had compared his level of influence to many of his predecessors, like Dr. Martin Luther King Jr., Moses, King David, and some say he was just like Christ. Now, we can all agree that he was not Jesus Christ himself. Yet it is our common goal as believers to be "*like* Christ." See like Christ in Luke 2:52, he had grown in wisdom, stature, and favor –with

> *Teach me, and I will hold my tongue: and cause me to understand wherein I have erred. (Job 6:24)*

men and with God. So, I'm sure you can imagine, the magnitude of the impact this accusation had on a man of such character. He was faced with a mountain so big that most of the society he dedicated his life to serving had scorned him, written him off, and pronounced his ministry dead on arrival.

Though he could have initially responded in anger and hostility, God gave him the strength to stand strong while facing brutal persecution and scrutiny with peace and wisdom. When we find ourselves standing in the face of opposition, God gets the glory when we trust Him and seek Him for direction first. It's never easy to stand idly and listen to the ugly untruth spoken about yourself. We are all human, so it's natural to become angry.

Still, when we walk in the grace and all-consuming love of God, we can endure the fire without losing our cool. I am not saying the church family did not weep, or that his heart was not broken. We all possess the power to show God's love towards our enemies as they are attacking us. Even Jesus, as he hung on the cross in the face of His accusers, mustered up the strength to look towards heaven and intercede on behalf of his accusers. He asked forgiveness for the very ones who drove the nails through his hands and feet.

What does God say about you? For every lie the enemy tells, respond with the truth found in God's word. It may not be what you feel like doing. It will not feel natural, but it is what you must do to regain power over your accusers. When somebody suggests to you that you are not *qualified*, you remind them that you are God's *chosen* vessel.

Read this excerpt from the message bible:

3-5You've already put in your time in that God-ignorant way of life, partying night after night, a drunken and profligate life. Now it's time to be done with it for good. Of course, your old friends don't understand why you don't join in with the old gang anymore. But you don't have to give an account to them. They're the ones who will be called on the carpet—and before God himself.

(1Peter4:3-5)

Those who can only recount the errors and mistakes of your past are not qualified to travel with you on this journey. Those who cannot look beyond your weaknesses and challenge you to develop your strengths will only present counterproductive relationships.

For example, as you give up on drinking, smoking, drugs, or sexual addictions, you must also separate yourself from those who are still participating. If you don't, their actions will always serve as temptation to take you back to where you were. When you are invited to take part in the party, you will most likely refuse the invitation. You have grown and made great strides towards a changed life. However, since they only see you as the person you used to be, these same people will begin to ridicule and cause you to feel ashamed for your desire to change. You will start to experience rejection from those who you spent so much of your life with.

See, ultimately, these people want you to regret your growth. This is counterproductive. You need the support of people who can understand where God has called you to go in your life and will hold you accountable for getting there. I have had to learn the long hard way that change in my life will 'almost never' be accepted by those who deny *a change in their own* lives. Normally that's where persecution is born; it's born deep down in the hearts of those who refuse to grow and change.

> *Therefore, I take pleasure in infirmities, in reproaches, in necessities, in persecutions, in distresses for Christ's sake: for when I am weak, then am I strong.*
> *(2 Corinthians 12:10 NKJV)*

Why is persecution so effective anyway? Well, studies show that we as human beings rely heavily upon the affirmations and approval of other human beings. That mindset is not created by God's design. Did you not know that before you were formed in your mother's womb (before she even considered the thought of you), God had already anointed, appointed, and affirmed you for *this journey* you are traveling? Therefore, you do not need the approval of others to walk in His promises. The idea of letting people go who only challenge your identity may be painful to embrace. However, it is crucial to our earthly experience, that we learn how to love them (in spite of their disapproval), thank them for their season in our lives, and move on to completing our assignment.

Read this excerpt from the message bible:

14-16If you're abused because of Christ, count yourself fortunate. It's the Spirit of God and His glory in you that brought you to the notice of others. If they're on you because you broke the law or disturbed the peace, that's a different matter. But if it's because you're a Christian, don't give it a second thought. Be proud of the distinguished status reflected in that name!
(1 Peter 4:14-16 The MSG)

It is very sobering to know that I am not obligated to fulfill other people's expectations of me. When people disapprove of God's work in your life, it is evident that they are demanding that you meet 'their' expectations of you. For example, people will at times expect you to become depressed after the loss of a job or a loved one. Yet, when you instead respond to the tragedy with increased insight into God's greater plan, this disappoints them. Upon their disappointment, you will begin to hear on the rumor mill, "*He /She thinks they're better than us.*"

The people from your past will expect you to remain at their level of maturity. When you don't meet that expectation, it is a mere reflection of their immaturity. Instead of frustrating yourself by trying to understand why you are not accepted anymore, I'll tell you again: "Love them and leave them alone." Here's food for thought: don't ever feel inferior when you are rejected by the crowd, God has called you to a higher standard of living. Believe it or not, later down the road, that same crowd will face storms that will drive them right back to you for a demonstration on how you made it.

You will never be able to please everybody or cause everybody you encounter to love or accept you. We all want to be liked, but that is not our ultimate goal. Even when we have embraced this and begin to walk in confidence, we may still find ourselves with more enemies than we can count. David said, "*Those who hate me without a cause are more than the hairs of my head*" (Psalm

69:4). Rest assured, when you count the entire kingdom of God, you will find that there are more standing with you than there are working against you. So, position yourself in comfort, knowing that you are *never* alone. You always have an army standing with you in the face of opposition.

> *Let the words of my mouth, and the meditation of my heart, be acceptable in thy sight, O LORD, my strength, and my redeemer.*
>
> *Psalm 19:14 (KJV)*

Once your belief in God's word and in the power you possess reaches a certain level of maturity, persecution will become the platform that propels you into your destiny. Spiritual maturity will require us to endure persecution, with class and with grace.

Therefore, it is crucial that we learn to sabotage the work of the enemy by using our own tongues for positive influence, empowerment, inspiration, edification, and exhortation. By responding to negative critics and naysayers with what comes natural, we are only fueling their fire and helping to fulfill their agendas. The last thing you will want to do is validate the accusations of your offenders. We as believers, cannot entertain criticism and then respond with more criticism. We must be wise and temperant like Esther standing before the king; becoming slow to speak and quick to listen.

Don't get me wrong, I totally understand how bad it hurts; the tears you swallow in pride are not unseen. In my life, I think I have encountered more ridicule and rejection than one could possibly endure. I understand what it takes to "maintain your composure" on the out-side –while battling fury and unearned shame on the inside. At one point, I felt like I had taken so much perse-cution that I began my own path to self-destruction. However, I discovered that persecution had pushed me down to my knees in prayer and then out to the forefront to speak life into others. As others found their entertain-ment in mocking my decisions for Christ, I grew more passionate about leading others who are hurting towards their own liberty. This is how my pain became my plat-form. The more negativity I encountered, the more frequently I said to God, "Send me, I'll go."

Read this excerpt from the message bible:

"Not only that—count yourselves blessed
every time people put you down or throw you out or speak lies
about you to discredit me. What it means is that the truth is
too close for comfort and they are uncomfortable. You can be
glad when that happens—give a cheer, even !—for though
they don't like it, I do ! And all heaven applauds. And know
that you are in good company. My prophets and witnesses
have always gotten into this kind of trouble.
(Matthew 5:11-12 The MSG)

Only the strong at heart and secure in Christ have the guts to go through such persecutions. It's not an easy task, and it is the road less traveled. Only the strong and selfless have the courage to pray for their enemies. These warriors have the *grit* to be humble.

Do you identify with this type of warrior? If so, then it is because of your faith in Him and your trust in His love for you –that you find peace in the face of lies, ridicule, and scorn.

Nobody knows like you know what it takes to be you. Many may profess that they know you, they may pretend to know what makes you happy, sad, or frustrated. At times, they may claim if they were in your shoes, they would handle things a different way. They may suggest to you that you've got things all wrong.

Still, I am here to assure you, only God can speak on the affairs of your life. Only He can see the intricate details of your situation. Only He can guide you through your storm, and bring you out with a posture of praise and a victorious testimony on the other side. So be relieved: no matter what people may say about you, they are clueless of the sum total of His works through you. They obviously have no idea how God feels about you. They cannot calculate your volume!

Overcoming persecution requires a heart that is confident and secure in the love of God; it requires a heart that is transformed to beat in sync with the sound of His word. It also requires a heart that's not easily offended. How many times have we overheard the negative words of someone whom we love and just wanted to run, hide, and utterly disappear? How many times have we pleaded our case among those we loved and begged them to understand our position or circumstances. Yet, despite our supplications, we still found ourselves slandered, rejected, and exiled?

I am a believer that every plan the enemy develops to harm me, God uses each of those plans to elevate me. Those very same words that were spoken to hurt you and bring you to your knees in shame, will only be used to strengthen your heart against future attacks.

I am learning daily that the more passionate you become about saving souls and leading the lost out of darkness, the more often you will be attacked. It just comes with the territory. So, the sooner we learn to live as evangelists allowing the negativity roll off our backs, the sooner we will gain momentum and advance to doing more significant works in the name of Christ.

At the cross in Calvary, Jesus hung there bloody dripping, sweaty, and pierced in his side. In his human nature, he would have loved to avoid this assignment. Yet still, He hung there, in agony and pain. He did not just suffer there from his own physical pain. He was also in pain emotionally for those who put him there.

Jesus knew that He was dying for the very ones who lied and crucified him. It was not easy at any point during that occasion for Christ to accept the rejection of humanity. It was not easy at any moment for Christ to embrace that He was giving his blood and all of life itself for the very ones who were assassinating him. After He had spoken life to the dead, restored sight to the blind, healed the sick, and brought joy to the brokenhearted, how could he end up here; publicly humiliated, naked, and ashamed? If only they had known who He was and why He had come.

As they completed this fatal crime against Jesus, they dipped a sponge in vinegar and offered it to our savior to quench His thirst. Yet he did not swallow the bitter drink. This is symbolic: instead of responding to his accusers and murderers with the bitterness they deserved, Christ looked towards heaven and asked the Father to "*Forgive them for they know not what they do.*" Those who reject Christ from their hearts, refuse to grow in character, and are looking for an excuse to justify their sin, will always rejoice when they see you, God's children, defeated. You can expect naysayers and counterfeits to show up at your crucifixion with a bitter sponge. They will not miss an opportunity to pour salt in your wounds. You may as well expect that. Rejection, scorn, and humiliation, I repeat, "It comes with the territory." They will say to one another, "See, I told you she wasn't all that!" Or "*Where is your God now?*"

I would love to tell you that everybody will lovingly come to your rescue. I'd love to tell you that people will empathize with your circumstances and offer their support. If I made that claim, I'd be lying. There will always be someone waiting to rush in and kick you when they see you down. Most times, it will be the person you least expected. However, do not allow your emotions and feelings draw you to a place of bitterness. Like Christ, you cannot come down from the cross. Like Christ, you cannot allow speculations about who you are or where you are going –get in the way of the promise God has for your life.

After spending years living a life that was aching from the wounds of abuse, I had to make up in my mind that I am no longer a victim. I am no longer running for my life, struggling to survive. I am a champion for Christ, and I will not retreat because of rejection or someone else's refusal to grow. I'm bold! I'm strong! I'm overcome by the blood of the Lamb!

Now in response to the verbal assassinations, negativity, and shame, do what you do best: S-M-I-L-E! Smile beyond the humiliation. Smile beyond the pain. Smile beyond the tears and know this one thing: nothing can ever separate you from the love of God. Not divorce, not abandonment; not the friends who secretly slander you, nor the family who left you for dead. No matter what happens and what is said, you will always have the love and commitment of God that He will never leave you alone. This is what *kept* Jesus on the cross. The covenant being created (between God and mankind) as a result of his blood being poured out, gave him peace in the process. Jesus knew there was greater glory in all that He endured. Jesus knew that by remaining on the cross, he gave fame and credibility to the Father. Jesus knew that his demise wasn't about him at all. When the assignment was completed, He would sit at the right side of the Father and smile. Christ would smile because by not giving in, he changed the fate of humanity. He smiled because it was his sacrifice that had now *conquered* sin and shame. It was his love that restored the broken-hearted. Christ smiled because, in His death, he gave us all LIFE.

Now, wait until they see *you* smiling. While the crowd is laughing unaware of God's plan to refine you, God is changing the scene all behind the curtain. He is dusting off the shame and erasing the tracks of your tears. Behind the scene when nobody is watching God is increasing your value.

God never intended for you to become a carbon copy of anybody else but Him. Your persecution is supplemental to His overall refining process. God is doing His best work in you. So, while He is working, wear the garment Christ left for all of us to wear, the garment of praise. You are a champion! The next time you hear a rumor or you find yourself persecuted for your decision to do what pleases God, remember, Christ has given you permission to square your shoulders, throw your head back, smile, and move forward. Yes! You have the authority to simply smile and rest in the grace of God. If God is for you, who can dare stand against you?! Today, make the decision that "Never again will I dine on the affections of others. I am stronger, I am better, and I am ready for whatever!"

But you are God's Chosen treasure –priests who are kings, a
spiritual "nation" set apart as God's devoted ones. He called
you out of darkness to experience His marvelous light, and
now he claims you as His very own. He did this so that you
would broadcast His glorious wonders throughout the world.
(1Peter 2:9 TPT)

*We are cast down
but never destroyed...
(2Corinthians 4:9)*

*We've been thrown down,
but we haven't broken.
(The Message)*

MOTIVATED TO
RISE AGAIN!

She said "Yes" to the ring. She said "Yes" to the dress. She said "YES" to the venue. She said "YES" to the cake. She said "YES" to the home. She said "YES" to the new life that awaited her at the altar. Sadly, in all her agreements, she unknowingly told God "NO."

After only a few months she would soon discover the consequences. The emotional turmoil would begin. The "fairytale-like" second chance she had believed for, unfolded as a nightmare. The romance and the honeymoon were over fast. The roses and gifts that once made her feel valued and special now turned her stomach each time they appeared. They would only show up now as restitution after she'd been abused.

The arguments, screams, and cries would only increase as his mental illness began to reveal itself. The woman had become like a sitting duck, vulnerable to every manic episode bound to occur. She finds herself afraid to fall asleep many nights, afraid to make him upset, afraid to disobey or disagree with him. Fearful of how far he could possibly take his anger. Mortified by his promise to humiliate her publicly. Petrified at the thought of being killed at the hands of her lover. "Will there come a time when he will act on the things he threatens?" she wonders. Her children beg her "Mom, please, let's leave."

Unwilling and afraid to admit to friends and family that she had made the same mistake twice, she clenched her fists and fought silently in fear and in pain for as long as she could. This would be the second time she had ignored the still small voice; she'd heard it the night before they arrived at the Justice of The Peace. Yet, her hope for a new family and a new life filled with love and unrelenting intimacy would not be fulfilled here either.

Her prayers for healing in this marriage would not come the way she wanted it to. Her healing in this marriage would only occur in the divorce. Her healing in this marriage would only occur once she had made up in her mind that this was "not God's will for my life after all." Her healing in this marriage would only come after repentance and starting the journey again –in a new direction.

Still, traumatized by the attacks, and overwhelmed with depression –she could not easily find the strength or the willpower to walk away. It was not easy for her to ignore the effects of his abusive behavior. So, she did what so many people lack the courage to do –she sought therapy.

There, in a dimlight office, on a leather couch, she embarked upon the will to pursue freedom. Soon enough, filled with shame and disappointment, she packed her children and their things and headed to safety.

It would take her much longer to process what has happened in such a short time. It would take 3 years to unclench her fists and release the disappointment, the shame, the wedding memories, the abandonment, and the self-sabotaging behaviors –finger by finger. It would take her a while to find the courage to pull her head out of the sand and come out of isolation. It would take years to stop hiding, and being tormented by the shame of what has happened. Still *thirsty for unconditional love and acceptance* she ignored the small voice that said STOP and found herself living out the consequences of her decision to say "YES" to an imposter.

So many (men and women) have traveled on this exact same journey. Thirsty, hungry, and needy for the only One who could fulfill our bankrupt souls –we have all fallen prey to narcissists, con-artists, and wolves in sheep clothing. We've all believed the empty promises. We've all been fooled by the "wooden nickel." At some time or another, each of us has surrendered to our own impatience and taken matters into our own hands.

Satan has already proven to us back in the Garden of Eden, that he has the innate ability to manipulate us into spending our lives chasing after the things we already possess. He did this to Eve first, by coercing her to eat from the "tree of knowledge of good and evil". He persuaded her by promising she would "become like God."

125

Sadly enough, she was not aware that she was *already* like Him – created in His image.

I am very aware that this is not a popular message. But I must go on to say that like a thirsty soul in the desert, we run towards the mirages –mistaking those things that make us thirsty for relief. We chase after things that we believe will add value to our lives – only to discover they are designed to reduce our standards and lower our expectations. We pursue relationships that we think we cannot live or breathe without –then painfully learn the person was sent to suffocate the life out of us. We have all in some way, lacked the patience to wait on that which is designed and approved by God. Instead, we have settled for what appears to be the next best thing –*the counterfeit.*

Furious with God and disappointed with myself for hoping again, only to find myself a victim of domestic abuse, I told myself quickly, "I'm not getting up anymore, I'm not believing in love anymore, I give up, I quit!" Like all of my other falls in life, after this fall I envisioned myself throwing in the towel, calling it quits, and making a life in this pit of despair. I began to isolate myself, as an attempt to escape from my humiliation. It's amazing to even me, that I can pen these thoughts and emotions to you dear reader. I must expose the fact that even Christians, (yes, children of God) get knocked down, and find themselves desperate for answers on how to get back up again. We bleed, cry, and get angry like the rest of the world. Turmoil does not discriminate, and we all have an equal opportunity to experience disappointment. We are not immortal, without feeling, or exempt from defeat, we are *merely redeemed.*

The first thing you must have, after falling or being knocked down in defeat, is a picture of "*what up looks like*" to motivate you. The images you replay in your mind are what will ultimately determine if you are able to recreate hope or if you die in defeat. Your brain is created with many capabilities.

First, it is designed with the ability to remember things of your past. Second, it is also developed with the ability to interpret the present. In addition, your brain also has the power to create an image of what tomorrow will look like. Some people call it fantasizing or day-dreaming. Truth be told, what your brain is doing after defeat, is creating a new reality.

This reminds me of the scientific definition of regeneration. Wikipedia states:

[9]"*In biology, regeneration is the process of renewal, restoration, and growth that makes genomes, cells, organisms, and ecosystems resilient to natural fluctuations or events that cause disturbance or damage.*"

There are certain organisms, like starfish, that if you cut off a part of it, that organism will take supply from the

---

[9] Source: https://en.wikipedia.org/wiki/Regeneration_(biology)
"In biology, regeneration is the process of renewal, restoration, and growth that makes genomes, cells, organisms, and ecosystems resilient to natural fluctuations or events that cause disturbance or damage."

remaining cells and recreate or regenerate that part of itself. This power also applies to our minds. When something in our minds, our dreams or ideas have been destroyed or cut off, our minds have the immediate capacity to pull from the cells remaining in our brains and *create a new dream*!

Also take note that the definition says, "regeneration produces resilience to disturbance or damage." Now there is an empowering fact. If you can just tap into the potential to regenerate a new mind, a new dream, a new perspective – you will become more resilient than before. What disturbed you and damaged you before –those circumstances cannot throw you off course anymore.

²It is like the precious ointment upon the head, that ran down upon the beard, even Aaron's beard: that went down to the skirts of his garments.

Psalm 133:2 KJV

Neuro-scientists have researched and discovered that thinking about something else (daydreaming or mind-wandering) blocks access to memories of the recent past. You must employ the part of your brain that can create an image of where you are going or want to be. You must allow that image to become more significant than the picture of your past or your current circumstances. As long as you allow where you have been or are right now to be brighter than the image of where you are going, you will never get up and move forward.

MOTIVATED TO RISE AGAIN!

Even though it hasn't happened yet, you must allow that image to become large enough redevelop hope. You may have just had your car repossessed, but you have got to get a glimpse of someone handing you a new set of keys! You may have lost your home, but you must grasp the image of planting roses in your new front yard. It may not be your current reality, but it is still possible. You can do all things with the strength of Christ in you!! You *can* get up. Your hope is in the Lord, so tell the enemy, "Get thee behind me Satan, I am GETTING UP!!!!"

Our minds may be tired, and we may feel defeated. But we cannot continue to operate from what we see in the natural. We must regenerate new mental images and begin living according to the reality that exists in our mind.

Scripture tells us that anointing oil is poured on at the head first, then runs down on the beard of Aaron, and continues to run down and collect at the edge or the hem of His garment. We know that one definition of anointing is that it is "the power of God that gives us the ability to manifest His presence in our lives."

The anointing has caused many miraculous wonders to occur. It was the anointing of God that assured the woman with the issue of blood that she would be healed of her infirmities. It was the anointing that gave Jesus the ability to lay hands on the dead, blind, and lame; causing each of them to be elevated from their lowest points in life.

In the Bible, we are told that holy anointing is poured out at the highest place, which is *the head,* and ends up at the lowest position... *the hem.* Contrarily, anointing power is generally demonstrated at the lowest position first. The power of God is not seen or activated at the most successful points of my life. Instead, it is more visible in the painful seasons. The anointing is not as appealing when all the bills are paid, and we are living the good life. It is neither effective when storms are nowhere in sight.

Rather, it is visible when there are fires all around me, the kids seem to have lost their minds, my job is failing me, my body is ailing with pain, and my enemies are surrounding me to laugh and criticize. It makes its debut when I don't have any answers to the problems. This is undoubtedly when the anointing has it's time to shine!

In the Bible, Proverbs 24:16, reminds us that "A righteous man falls seven times, but he gets back up again." I used to wonder God "Why me? Why am I always the one going down for the count? As soon as I regain my strength to stand again here comes another blow that knocks me off my feet? Why can't I ever get a break, there is always something traumatic happening my life??" It was during this season of my life, and as I am writing this chapter of the book that God answered that life-long question. God says, "I trust you with storms."

Be careful how you judge those who appear to be always going through a storm. Be careful how you praise those who seem to always have it all together. Some people lack self-control, are poor stewards of their resources, and ultimately wind up in distress. Then, there are *some* people who God trusts to be knocked down, repeatedly. They will always encounter unexpected drama, unexpected storms, and unexpected failure. This is because God trusts them with the *unexpected.* He knows how they will respond, He knows they will arise each time and bring Him glory. He knows that His anointing is in them; His hand is on them. So be very cautious of judging or criticizing those who always appear to be going through the fire, for they are heavily anointed. These are God's Champions!

The bible clearly warns, *"Touch not my anointed and do my prophet no harm" (1Chron. 16:22)* God is the source of their strength. And since the anointed can smell rain before it begins to fall, and can sense a storm before the thunder rolls, they grab hold of Him and brace themselves to ride it out. They do this knowing that the anointing to endure will secure them—keeping them from being swept out to sea!!

Furthermore, after each storm, God's anointing will restore you to your original beautiful state. God, who is covered in splendor, makes it His business to beautify the meek. After surviving years of domestic violence as a young woman, I had no idea I would then many years later have to suffer the agony of being rejected and then abandoned by my 1st husband. I never expected to spend countless nights crying and pacing the floor wondering where he was. I never expected to be disfigured by emotional distress lose the glow of joy from my face. I never expected him to *leave*. After enduring emotional abuse in my 2nd marriage, it was only the anointing power of God that replaced my ashes of mourning with a garment of praise.

It was God's anointing that rejuvenated my broken spirit after enduring the unexpected. It was the anointing that filled my heart with worship again. It was the anointing that restored the gleam of HOPE back into my eyes. When I stare in the mirror now, I no longer see the effects of abuse and abandonment. I no longer see disfiguration and stress in my face. Instead, I can see the young girl filled with passion and expectancy. She is full of life and hope. She is dreaming of paradise. I can once again gaze into the mirror and recognize the glory of God. His illuminating spirit resonates from within me!

It's never easy to shake off defeat and rise to your feet again. Rocky Balboa, in his final rendition of the "Rocky" series, makes a declaration to his son that shapes and defines his entire career of fighting. He quotes,[10]"Life is not about how hard you get hit, it's about how hard of a hit you can take and get back up again!"

God has called many of us to be knocked down, thrown down, and defeated. We then find ourselves in a

---

[10] Source: Movie: ROCKY "Life is not about how hard you get hit, it's about how hard of a hit you can take and get back up again!"

place that we have never been before. Sickness? Jobless? Divorce? Abandonment? Depression? Abuse? Public humiliation? I had never been bound by so much at once. Once you find yourself down in the valley, and you begin to look around in this unfamiliar place—you wonder, "God what do I do next? How do I get back up from here?

Things do not look the same; people who I used to depend on are unreachable. The ideas that got me to where I am today are now obsolete." In that very moment, you will hear a voice to help you start the resurgence, "*Remember not the former things—nor consider the things of old!!*"

Fortunately, God would not have us to repeat the route that brought us to where we are to-

> *Remember ye, not the former things, neither consider the things of old Behold, I will do a new thing; now it shall spring forth; shall ye not know it? I will even make a way in the wilderness, and rivers in the desert.*
>
> *(Isaiah 43:18-19 KJV)*

day. That would be considered insanity; doing the exact same thing, but expecting a different result. Newsflash: we do not serve an insane God! He is taking us *all* in a new direction, which leads us up and out of this valley. Though the journey may be painful and we may not be ready to walk it out, we must not stay here. Our future selves are relying upon our current ability to release yesterday's hurts, look beyond today's uncertainties, and launch forward into a new day!

Isaiah 43:18 tells us in summary that when we are anointed to get back up again, God will take us in a new direction and we will end up in a place we have never seen before. This may mean that we are headed towards a path that has never been carved, and on a road that has never been traveled. This may mean that we will be traveling in the dark for a while. Still, God knows the way that we are to take, and He will not cause our foot to stumble.

Therefore, when we cannot trace Him, we can surely trust Him! We can surely trust in the Lord with all our hearts and lean not to our own understanding (Proverbs 4:5-7). We can surely acknowledge Him in all our ways, and He will surely direct our paths. He will show us where to drink and be filled; where to step, and where to rest. He will not leave us alone.

Rising above the things that knock us down require more forgiving and forgetting than anything else. Unforgiveness is a heavyweight that has the power to hold down the strongest of people. It can be compared to an anchor. If unforgiveness lands with you when you fall, you will not move again. Unforgiveness is a sure way to remain defeated after being knocked down. As long as you are anchored in unforgiveness, you will not experience the anointing to rise up again. You may say, "You don't know how bad that woman hurt me." "How can I forgive the man who abused me?" "How can I forgive the person who murdered my child?" Or even, "How can I forgive my father who raped me?" But I promise you

MOTIVATED TO RISE AGAIN!

(and you can rest on the idea) that God will *anoint* you to forgive once you make a *choice* to forgive.

Some forgiveness is only achieved by the power of His spirit. God knows you don't have the strength to release some things on your own. He will not force you to forgive the offense. Still, if you love Him like you say you do, then you have the power of God *in you* to love and forgive those who have disappointed you. If you are indeed one with Christ, then you possess His strength to forgive. Releasing what has happened to us is never an easy task; just like it was not easy for Christ to forgive us, over and over again, as he hung on the cross and died. The sacrifice of Christ not only redeems us. But it also gives us the will and courage to forgive the unforgivable. His sacrifice anoints us with the grace to forgive like He forgave.

The Apostle Paul's advice for rising above our present-day *circumstance* is simple: "Let go of yesterday and reach for tomorrow." That sounds easy in theory. However, in the application we have all too many times found ourselves arrested in the *"would haves"* and *"should haves"* of our past. Paul was demonstrating to all of us the ability to forget the failures and disappointments behind us and grab hold of the promises that are relevant for today.

> *Brethren, I count not myself to have apprehended: but this one thing I do, forgetting those things which are behind, and reaching forth unto those things which are before.*
>
> *(Philippians 3:13)*

After several interviews with a company I worked for many years ago, I found myself in prayer one morning asking God, "Show me why I am not moving forward. I mean, I know that the door to abundance has been opened for me. I know that I am the head and not the tail. I know that I am *supposed to be* a lender and not a borrower. I even recognize that there is nothing in front of me blocking me from crossing over."

Now, His answer was a hard pill to swallow. Still, when God speaks and gives you an answer, for some reason you feel better by seeing the light, whether what you see is good or bad. Nobody likes to be in darkness. When I got silent and still enough to hear His voice, this is what I heard, "Close the doors behind you."

It came so unexpectedly that I almost tripped over the convicting word as I ended my prayer. But as I started my day, I kept hearing it, "Close the doors behind you." When I got in my car, I heard the voice again, "Close the doors behind you." I soon envisioned myself standing in-between the past and my future, a dark and low place with doors to both paths swinging open.

The door ahead of me leading to my future seemed to cast off this bright light and was blowing a fresh, clean wind. In the doorway behind me leading to my past, I felt a stale draft. This side appeared dreary, full of chaos, questions, and busy. Now, picture yourself there. Ask yourself this question: "If both doors are open and they both are exerting equal force in an attempt to draw you in, guess which direction you are going in?" Neither! I said "Wow! Okay, God, I hear you."

On my way to work that morning, I recognized that recently there had been a lot of old acquaintances, old habits, and old attitudes that had been cleverly creeping their way back into my life. It was not that I had lost sight of my goals; it surely was not that my identity in Christ had been distorted. Yet, this state of mind I encountered was just enough to distract me from moving forward.

I found out that sometimes, I allowed people to hold me hostage to being the old Kim. Being "held hostage" means the changes in my character were not acceptable by others who knew the old me. So, when I attempted to approach old relationships with a changed perspective, I experienced rejection, jealousy, and many times conflict. As a result, I wavered between being the new me and accommodating others who were not comfortable with my change.

Once you have decided to cross all the way over and put your life in God's hands, you will discover that everything begins to change suddenly. You start to notice that the people who were comfortable with you, when you were "messed up," are now less tolerable of you —now that you are getting it together.

Likewise, you will also become less tolerant of relationships that don't complement where God is taking you. You become less comfortable with handling situations with the same old mindset. This frustration will force you to transform into the person God originally intended you to be.

Sometimes, your transformation will only be visible to you and God. When you are growing and have transformed into an entirely new creature, it's disappointing when nobody recognizes it. When you have been washed and cleansed of your sins, you want the world to acknowledge your new attire. It's like getting a new expensive suit. When you can finally afford to clean up well, you are ready to go out strolling on the town –for everyone to be in awe when you pass by. That is perfectly ok. Still, *some* things must be hidden and nurtured in our hearts for a season.

Just remember this, no matter what people around you are saying, agree with the Father and only His report. His love for us draws us closer to Him, and we are accountable to Him. So, if He says NO to a proposal, our answer is NO! If He says NO to a conversation, our answer is NO! If He says NO to a relationship, our answer is NO! Each time we say "NO!" we are closing the doors behind us. It's time to rise up from this place and head in a new direction. Let's move on from here. Let's run this race to the end.

A true athlete will be disciplined in every respect, practicing constant self-control in order to win a laurel wreath that quickly withers. But we run our race to win a victor's crown that will last forever!
(1 Corinthians 9:25)

One day long ago, God's Word came to
Jonah, Amittai's son: "Up on your feet and
on your way to the big city of Nineveh!
Preach to them. They're in a bad way, and I
can't ignore it any longer." However, Jonah
got up and went the other direction to Tar-
shish, running away from God. He went
down to the port of Joppa and found a ship
headed for Tarshish. He paid the fare and
went on board, joining those going to Tar-
shish—as far away from God as he could
get. (Jonah 1:1-3 The Message)

FROM WRESTLING
TO RESTING

---

*N*ow, how many times has God given you a command, and you reasoned with Him until you talked yourself out of following His instructions? Each of us has encountered the "sometimes inconvenient" instructions of God. So, like Jonah, we may do whatever we can to get as far away from the voice of God as possible. We may figure it's not the right time, we might not feel adequate, or we may want to do things our way. However, at the end of the day it's not about what we want that matters, it's about Him.

Jonah, whose name means "*dove,*" was the son of Amittai, which means in Hebrew, "*My Truth.*" The dove is the symbolic representation of the Holy Spirit. I find it quite interesting that Jonah was the son of a man named after, *the truth*. Jonah was the seed of truth. Amittai (the truth), brought forth Jonah, (dove/ Holy Spirit). It is clear here that God was sending His spirit, the Holy Spirit, to the people of Ninevah. These people were in darkness and in sin. They were living a cultural lifestyle apart from God's will. They, very much like us, needed the guidance and preservation of the Holy Spirit to bring them back into alignment with God.

I am the Way, the truth, and the Life. No one comes to the Father except through union with me. To know me is to know my Father too.

(John 14:6 TPT)

When Jesus was sent here to earth, he was sent here bearing *the truth*. When he came, he came to leave us with the Holy Spirit to guide us, keep us, and comfort us. As humans, we were here on earth living our lives in darkness. Moreover, because of this darkness, we were wholly disconnected from the Father.

Through Christ God saw fit to bring us the light of His word in truth. The truth is that we are not helpless slaves to sin, but we are joint heirs with Christ, a royal priesthood, God's own chosen people. That mean's we have the power to resist every temptation presented by the enemy.

So, what does this wrestling resemble? What does it mean to wrestle with God? In this instance, wrestling means we are going back and forth with Him. It also means we are trying to exert our will over His. Wrestling with God may resemble something like this: As God begins to close doors to the paths that lead us away from the journey he has designed for us, we fight against Him by forcing those doors back open (instead of allowing God to transform our lives).

We somehow get the idea that we can negotiate with Him by holding on to people, things, and agendas that don't line up with His plan for us. When He is directing us to change our way of thinking and our circles of influence, it's easy to conjure up convenient reasons, or might I say "excuses," to disobey His instructions.

For where your treasure is, there will your heart be also.

   (Matthew 6:21 KJV)

Then said Jesus unto his disciples, If any man will come after me, let him deny himself, and take up his cross, and follow me.

   (Matthew 16:21 KJV)

I can recall many years ago I developed a fetish for Coach handbags. I loved their smell. I loved the colors. Moreover, I relished the idea that the average person around me couldn't just walk in the store and purchase these handbags unless they were found in a discount store. Looking back in retrospect, I had secretly become reliant upon material possessions as a sense of self-worth. After I left the company that afforded me such luxury, I still had a closet full of these prized bags. On my new job, there was a woman who was less fortunate. She had a reputation for being somewhat bitter and having a negative attitude.

Well, one day I walked in carrying one of my prize bags. As I walked by, she turned around from her cubicle and complimented me saying, "Oh I love that bag!" Startled by her compliment, I smiled, thanked her and kept walking. When I got to my seat, I heard this frustrating voice that kept nagging at me, "Give her the bag." Now my initial thoughts were, "But why? She always negative towards me, and she doesn't even deserve it." Also, I knew for a fact that she had been spreading rumors about me. So why would I give away one of my most expensive items to someone who clearly did not like me?

I wrestled with this too long. God had made His instructions clear. It wasn't about me, but He wanted me to add value to *her* life by demonstrating *love*. However, I attempted futilely to find an excuse to disobey the instruction.

Coincidentally, just the day before I had switched purses while driving and therefore I still had another purse out in my car. I was tired of hearing the voice, so I gave in. I went out to my car, changed purses, and brought the prize bag back into the office empty. God had me to walk right up to her (with a spirit of humility) and say, "I want you to have this, enjoy your new bag." The look on her face was first amazement and then excitement. She could barely find the words to say Thank you.

When we wrestle with God's instructions, it reveals to us the nature of our hearts. Our motives and idolatry of 'self' are exposed. *Self* will always seek to be in control. *Self*-wants to have the last say in everything. *Self*-wants to win. *Self*-wants to be recognized. Ultimately, *Self*-wants a platform to be exalted. Once we give in to *Self*, *Self* becomes our lord. This mindset of self-lording is a demonstration of idolatry.

If you will recall, the first of the ten commandments informs us that God is a jealous God and would have no other gods before Him; this includes the god of *self (Exodus 20-3)*. He is the potter, and we are the clay. The goal He has in mind is to mold and refine us to reflect the purest and most flawless image of Him; in all our ways. In tandem, our spirit of *self* will fight to have its own image/identity every step of the way.

Because we are human, it is our nature to seek the fulfillment of our desires. We will be willing to pursue that fulfillment even if it means disobeying God's will and hurting those we love. Our flesh will always disagree with the Spirit of God. As the Holy Spirit compels us to obey His will, our human nature will continue to compete by pulling us in the opposite direction. As long as we have breath in our bodies, we will be subject to spiritual training. We must learn to deny our carnality and instead make the decision to go after what matters most to Him – *whether we want to or not.*

When He recognizes that the desires of our hearts do not correspond with His, then the Father will present an opportunity for us to examine ourselves. God will first examine us to expose areas in which we need to grow; examination reveals our areas of weakness. The results of our self-examinations are most reliable when we measure our thoughts and actions against those of the righteous men and women found in the Bible. When our self-examinations are complete, the areas of our lives that God desires for us to reconcile with Him will become apparent to us.

We also wrestle when we face an unexpected tragedy. You might have experienced the loss of a job which forces you into poverty and standing in line for government assistance. Like me, you may have experienced divorce which forces you into a life of uncertainty. You may have spent your entire life trying to prove to your enemies and those who have picked on you that you are worth more then they have classified you to be. However, while we are wasting time attempting to prove our naysayers wrong, God is waiting for us to let it go. In each of these scenarios, He wants to use our tragedies to transport us onto the path He originally intended for us.

Others may have criticized you, but He allowed you to have that experience so that you could be an an impactful advocate for teens and young adults. There may be a non-profit organization in your future from which you are to help teens and young adults learn how to create a positive self-image.

You might have experienced divorce and are now a single parent. Singles, often feeling pressured by loneliness and the need for financial security, many times enter marriage for the wrong reasons. Many are hungry for answers on how to become self-confident in their singleness. Did you consider that maybe He has allowed you to endure that experience with divorce so that as a result you would become a signpost pointing towards hope?

You might have experienced job loss or a shattered career. Consider this: even in a job loss, your sudden tragedy may have been intended just so that you would recognize your potential to launch a successful business. Don't ever knock the idea that you have the potential to become the next household name.

Many years ago, I lead a ministry team as we served in homeless shelters on a monthly basis. There was one woman, Susan who was always very humble. She is a quiet and softspoken woman. However, she was very eager to serve. Many years ago, Susan was diagnosed with breast cancer. She doesn't mind me sharing her testimony. Susan was already in a financially desperate situation as she lived with relatives. As she served, I continued to pray for her and encourage her in her season of unemployment. Then, when she announced her diagnosis to me, I was heartbroken. I kept asking God, what is it you are doing in Susan's life? Weren't matters already desperate enough for her? In her storm, Susan demonstrated resilience. She showed me a faith I had never witnessed.

Each time I would see Susan in service worshipping, I would be in amazement at just how strong she was. I would approach her to speak and embrace her, sometimes she would fight to hold back her tears, but her strong response was always, "I am *ALREADY* healed!" She had a definite swagger as she emphasized *already*. I had only heard of the incredible strength and resilience of cancer patients. Still, I was in awe as I witnessed this woman in the midst of her circumstances. She was standing, facing, and beating the odds, with only her faith. I was left speechless after each encounter with her.

When God wants to take us in a new direction, naturally, we resist because we have gotten comfortable and conditioned for the path we are already on. As humans, we don't like things to be shaken up in our lives. We love knowing what to expect so we can be prepared to respond accordingly. So, when God wants to move us, He usually has to snatch things and people from us unexpectedly to push us into the next phase. The good thing about this is knowing that He only does this to those He can trust with a crisis.

God is wise and all knowing. Therefore, He will not bring you to a place of tragedy if He knows that you are not strong enough to endure it. Our Heavenly Father would not have brought Job to his demise if He weren't convinced that Job would ultimately come through the fire unscathed. In the same way that He was fully aware of every step along Job's journey, He is fully engaged in your trip through this earthly experience. Your heavenly Father is certain of the routes you will choose, and the mistakes you will make. We may make faulty decisions on our own at times, but He will not cause your feet to stumble. When we are sensitive to His plan, and willing follow His lead, God is careful enough to keep us and protect us, even in a crisis. He already knows how we will turn out.

Typically, our wrestling begins when God leads us to a path that will take us out of our comfort zone. We wrestle with God when we are forced to "*change*" (and that's never a tasty word to chew). We wrestle when we feel the pain of being

But He knows the way that I take when He has tested me as I shall come forth as gold.

(Job 23:10)

stretched beyond our standard capacity to perform. We always experience discomfort when God reveals the characteristics, behaviors, and mindsets that we need to improve. It might be our heart, it might be our mind, or it might be our broken soul. Sometimes, there are bad habits He wants to destroy.

Moreover, when God is working on us, it can be compared to going through open heart surgery, *while awake*! Now, who in their right mind would enter an operation awake? It's never His intention to harm us. He wants to remove our calloused heart and replace it with a heart that matches the tenderness of His own. Ultimately, He wants us to grow. So, as I have mentioned before He does not need, nor will He ask us for our permission. He is God Almighty and when He is ready for us to change; we must brace ourselves for an irreversible "change."

As we look at the news (and right out our front doors), we can clearly see that the days in which we live are consumed with tragedy and for many an uncertain outcome. Our hearts become conditioned for constant disappointment and trauma. As a result, it is typical to find that our hearts have become hardened or calloused.

147

> While it is said, "To-day if ye will hear his voice, *harden not your hearts*, as in the rebellion."
>
> (Hebrews 3:8 NKJV)

Webster's definition of calloused is "*a*: being hardened and thickened *b*: feeling no emotion." A *callus* is an especially toughened area of skin which has become relatively thick and hard in response to *repeated friction, pressure, or other irritation*. Calluses are generally not harmful, but may sometimes lead to other problems, such as skin ulceration or infection.

Here are some things that can cause repeated friction, pressure, and irritation to our hearts:

1. Repeated failed relationships
2. Repeated rejection by friends and family
3. Remaining in toxic or abusive relationships
4. Disappointments
5. Starting projects but never completing them because of the fear of failure.

I must dig a little deeper and suggest to you that being calloused is also caused by a constant thirst or desire for something that seems to be unattainable. Like our calloused feet may desire water, moisture, rest, single people may desire an intimate relationship with the opposite sex. Children may desire attention and acceptance from their peers. Men and women both desire praise, recognition, and a sense of achievement. Finally, we all have a thirst and desire to experience the four-letter word LOVE.

When we are in pursuit of having these essential needs met and still come up empty-handed, it is understandable that our hearts can become calloused towards God. As a result, when He begins to reveal a new thing to us, we begin to wrestle with Him. Many times, like little children, we want *"our way."*

Jeremiah 17:9 reads:

The heart is deceitful above all things,
and desperately wicked: who can know it?

My spiritual father used to remind us often that "Satan cannot kill you. Nor can he stop the work of God in your life, but his best weapon is to DISTRACT you. If you allow him to succeed his distractions will greatly hinder your journey."

When we continuously strive to obtain the things we desire in our strength, it becomes harder to hear the voice of God. We cannot identify with God's voice because we are more focused on the things that we desire. In this present age, many of us suffer from the inability to determine which paths to take. So, the scripture says, "Today if ye will hear His voice, *harden not your hearts* as they did in the wilderness."

The Israelites were more focused on the things they felt they deserved and desperately needed, so they could not discern what the Father was doing in their lives. They lost their direction and track of time; causing them to wander in the desert for 40 years.

So likewise, when it seems as if that thing we want is out of our reach, when we can't seem to reach the things we are thirsty for, we get distracted by the lack of it. We then miss God's plan by making careless mistakes; ultimately causing our hearts to become hardened and calloused.

I think we can understand now what God meant when spoke in Ezekiel 36:26:

"A new heart also will I give you, and a new spirit will I put within you: and I will take away the stony heart out of your flesh, and I will give you a heart of flesh."

As God removes the heart of stone, we can indeed enter into a place of worship. During worship, God examines the desires of our hearts. Above all of our actions, abilities, and words, He sees the condition of our heart. When He determines that it is calloused, He will draw us to a place of worship, by which He softens our heart.

When we get a preview of His heart's desire for our lives, our hearts become softened and receptive to His pressing. Once our hearts have grown susceptible to His ways, He has the capacity to mold it to reflect the condition of His own. During this season of worship, God molds our heart so that we will learn to desire His will. Finally, through worship, we begin to *rest* in His will.

Sometimes God places us in circumstances that force us to make some painful decisions. When we attempt to avoid having to make the decision, we normally find that we are only causing greater pain. And not just to ourselves –but also to those who love us. Of course, those who are close to us would want nothing more than to help us see our dreams fulfilled. However, when we have clearly heard from God like Jonah did, and yet instead we choose to resist following His plans for us, everyone who is traveling with us will ultimately get caught in our storm.

As we set out to accomplish a goal that is not a part of God's plan, we will almost always find ourselves in a storm. It does not matter how smart you are, how much experience you may have, or how sound the business plan is; if it's not His will, you will find that the doors you expected to be open, have been nailed tightly shut! You won't be able to explain your seeming failure.

When you set out to do something, it is always wise to wait for guidance from the Holy Spirit before you begin to work. Without the help of God, we will always find ourselves overwhelmed, stressed out, and tired. We can attempt to pursue success, employing all the methods we learned in school –we can even network through hundreds of people. Still, if the goal is not God's goal, the plan will not work!

> *Going a little ahead, Jesus fell on his face, praying, "My Father, if there is any way, get me out of this. But please, not what I want. You, what do you want."*
>
> **Matthew 26:39**
> **The Message Bible**

Contrarily, when we choose to do things His way, whether we agree or not, He releases His favor and grace to complete His commands without being worn out. God prepares the way and does all the work for you. Even if you are in a hopeless and desert-like situation, *God's* purpose for your life shall be fulfilled! He will cause things to happen and doors to open for you that you could not have imagined. When you are in alignment with His plan, all you need is a humble heart, obedience, and the capacity to show up!

In the bible story, the men who were on the ship endured a great storm because Jonah was wrestling with God. After the crew spent all their energy praying to their idol gods, and throwing cargo off the ship to lighten the load, they soon realized that somebody had brought a curse upon the ship. Even the other passengers on the boat could recognize that they were not in control. A much greater Force was in control of this storm.

Once all of their gods failed to relieve them, they find Jonah at the bottom of the ship, asleep in the storm; a storm *he* created! I've always found this story extremely comical. Now, I could lecture you all day about being careful whom you allow to board your ship. Fortunately, that's a chapter all by itself! So, I will reiterate: *Some storms you encounter may not even belong to you. Therefore, use keen discernment when allowing passengers to board your ship.*

The crew realized their gods were useless. So, they summoned Jonah to seek help from *his* God. Finally, after pulling straws to determine who the guilty person was, it was revealed that Jonah was running from *his* God. They were surprised to discover that he had caused everyone on board to become engaged in this wrestling match between him and *his* God.

Like Jonah, ultimately, we will get to the place where we get tired of wrestling. Once we become exasperated, we ask ourselves, "Who was I to think I could wrestle with God, and stand a chance at winning?" He will get His way one way or the other. When we exhaust all our schemes and efforts, we will say, "I have no other ideas, no other recourse, I have exhausted all my energy, I'm tired of trying, I give up!" So like Jonah,

But Jacob stayed behind by himself, and a man wrestled with him until daybreak. When the man saw that he couldn't get the best of Jacob as they wrestled, he deliberately threw Jacob's hip out of joint. The man said, "Let me go; it's daybreak." Jacob said, "I'm not letting you go 'til you bless me." The man said, "What's your name?" He answered, "Jacob." The man said, "But no longer. Your name is no longer Jacob. From now on it's Israel (God-Wrestler); you've wrestled with God, and you've come through."

(Genesis 32: 24-28 The Message Bible)

we leave our failed course and jump ship to bring the storm to a cease.

In the last chapter, I shared a personal story with you about how after enduring seven weeks of a personal calamity, I finally gave in to the traumatic disappointments and said, "I give up." Did you notice how it was not until after I stopped wrestling with God's plan, and stopped trying to pursue my own agenda that the doors began to open for me? I had interviewed for a promising opportunity two months prior. Then, the day I expected to get an email or a call with a job offer, the door abruptly slammed shut instead. The hiring manager told me, "I'm sorry Kimberly; our corporate office decided we are not able to hire anyone right now." I was devastated and overwhelmed with disappointment. Consequently, after I gave up my fight with God, two months later, suddenly and unexpectedly, they called me back and said, "Our corporate office has opened the position for us to hire again and they have already signed off on the approval for us to hire you!"

As Jacob wrestled with the angel of the God, he was wrestling with the truth. Over the span of Jacob's life, he lived up to the meaning of his name. Jacob's name meant "heel-catcher." Jacob was a twin, and as he was being born, instead of pressing his way through the birth canal, he caught the heel of his brother and rode the easy way out of Rebekah's womb. Here, even I see Jacob as "*the opportunist.*" He would continue to seek the easiest way of getting things done with as little work on his part as possible.

Over the course of his life, Jacob secured himself by creating a circle of influence that would bring him rewards. Many considered him to be a trickster and a deceiver. On several occasions, he proved his accusers right. The Bible tells us that Jacob was a mild-mannered man. He did not follow the tradition of most men and become a hunter. Jacob captured the affection of his mother and influenced her to domesticate him. While Esau remained in the fields hunting, Jacob remained home in the tent with her. He even learned to cook! Imagine that! While his brother stayed out in the hot fields hunting for food and caring for the flocks, Jacob is back at the tent "chilling" in the kitchen with his mother.

Jacob performs his greatest stunt when he influences his brother to sell him his birthright for a bowl of soup. Tired and weary out of his mind from his work, Esau would have done anything for relief. Unfortunately, Brother Jacob does not miss the opportunity to take full advantage of the moment. Here once again, He was manipulating the situation to get the highest reward while doing as little work as possible. While Esau spent his days working to prove himself worthy of the birthright from his father, Jacob would snatch the blessing and reap the rewards without doing any work at all.

As he cleverly managed to build a life full of blessings by influencing and manipulating others, Jacob became very confident and secure in the life he had created for himself. Though he came out of the womb second, he did not waste any time in letting us know "I am a leader, and I will achieve greatness –*by any means necessary*!"

God had a plan to use Jacob's leadership. Still, even though He had an idea to put his leadership skills to good use, He also had a plan to *correct his faulty thinking* first. Though many leaders have significant influence and communication skills, for God to use them, they must first go through the process of being corrected.

Jacob first manipulated his way out of the womb; He then captured His mother's affection. He cons his brother Esau out of the first-born birthright. Later, Jacob deceives his Father Isaac, to steal Esau's blessing. God knew that to begin the process of cleansing his deceitful characteristics, he would have to break Jacob's heart by allowing him to become a recipient of deceit himself. You reap what you sow –*it is inevitable.*

Though Jacob managed to manipulate his brother's birthright and steal his blessing, he was paying a heavy price for it—a life filled with drama! If you study his story, you will notice that at every turn, he found himself wrestling with other deceivers for what was rightfully his. After Jacob had formed his own family and was now doing all the "work" that came along with having a family, he desperately wanted to return home. However, on His journey there he also wrestled with the plan God had for his life.

As he tried to figure out how to return to his father's house, without being killed by his brother's army, once again he turned to his gift of influence. He decided to send his servants armed with lavish gifts and words of affection ahead of him. He figured, "I will manipulate my brother's anger, and then he will open his arms to receive me." Then the Lord showed up!

As He was left alone, the Angel of the Lord appeared and began to wrestle with Jacob. Scripture says, "He wrestled with a man until the breaking of day." I want to suggest to you that Jacob wrestled in the spirit first, then in the natural. The wrestling began as Jacob discovered that he was in the darkest moment of his life. Jacob had been on the run from his brother and then spent 14 years working for the woman he loved. He spent another six years working in the field and tending to his uncle's flock. A life of hard labor was a life we know Jacob was not accustomed to living.

So, for all 20 years, he wrestled with God as he was being forced to examine himself. He was fighting with the truth that he had brought the life of drama upon himself when he deceived his family back home. Jacob spent 20 years wrestling with the reality that he was reaping a harvest of deceit. He knew deep down inside he had sown just that.

Now, he's had enough and is ready to go home. As he made up his mind to go back and make things right, it's now the breaking of *day*. Jacob is coming out of the darkness and moving towards the light. Here, we can witness a physical manifestation of his spiritual battles. The angel touched the socket of Jacob's hip and left him permanently wounded. This wound would be Jacob's constant reminder of *the truth*.

When the angel asked him, "What is your name?" he wanted Jacob to tell the truth. Jacob had been asked this once before by his father. Being the deceiver that he was, Jacob lied and stole the blessing of his brother. He demonstrated to us that by posing as his brother and walking in his brother's blessing, he had negated the rightful blessing that was intended for him. Be careful how you desire to be blessed the way God blesses other people. Don't ever look at somebody else's blessing and say, "That should have been me!"

I used to watch a popular reality show on television, "The Wife Swap." I could not understand how the women could agree to go and live in another woman's home and become responsible for raising and cleaning up after another family. When we get in somebody else's lane, we also become responsible for the struggles that come along with their journey. I don't know about you, but I think there is enough trouble in this life without the added stress of someone's else's drama. Furthermore, when we take on storms and battles that were not intended for us, we are not anointed or equipped to survive them. God does not have to bring us through them.

So, this time as Jacob tells the truth and gives him his rightful name, Jacob, the Angel of the Lord released the blessing that was intended just for him. He is no longer Jacob but now Israel. He is no longer considered the heel-catcher, deceiver, and trickster; God has broken Jacob, and he has prevailed. God can use his gift of influence to raise and rule the 12 tribes of Israel. That's what his name now means; "*He will rule.*"

Many times, we are wrestling because we are so accustomed to living a lie that when the truth presents itself, we cannot bear it. Our hearts are simply not open or have no room at all to receive it. So, we go through periods of wrestling as we learn to allow God to open our heart, purge us, and make room for the power of His truth. Scripture tells us we cannot put *new wine* in old wineskins; for if we do the skin would burst and the new wine would be wasted. This *new wine* is a symbol of *new joy*; a new life, a new way of thinking and living. Old wineskins represent the *old way (the old you)*.

Think about this, what would happen if God gave a million dollars to someone with the mindset of poverty and government assistance? Instead of investing the million, leaving an inheritance for generations to come, and preparing for kingdom advancement, that person would most likely spend it all on houses, clothes, and material things with nothing left to show for it. That, of course, would be wasting the wine. During this time when we are wrestling, God fighting to give us new wineskins; a new way of thinking, a new lifestyle, and a new set of friends.

When we wrestle with God, an internal uprising occurs. We begin to experience the disagreement of our hearts and minds. This disagreement arises when *'who we are becoming'* produces the pain of letting go of *'who we were'*.

I don't know why we like to pretend like we have it all together, but spiritual transformation is a challenge for all Christians. When we are self-motivated to endure personal growth, *we have surrendere*d to the potter's hands. We have said to ourselves and the Master, "Yes I am willing and ready to have my flaws exposed –only for You to make me over again!"

Self-exposure takes both courage and character. Neither our friends nor our relatives can provide an answer or solution to the level of discomfort we feel at this stage of our Christian journey. When God begins to rectify the errors in our souls and remove our destructive thought patterns, it is tough to articulate the battle that is going on inside of you. You are in the surgery room surrendering to every incision from the surgeon's scalpel. You're experiencing lacerations known by only you and the surgeon.

You might feel as though you are having an out of body experience; where there are not just one, but two of you looking in the mirror. When that call to "change" coming from the inside of you, becomes louder than your audible voice, the fight to exist as you were begins. That sound inside of you is the voice of truth. The voice of truth is fighting against your past, your motives, your insecurities, and your fears. That voice of truth is calling you to experience a closer relationship with God. That voice of truth may be trying to release you from being satisfied with being an employee and empowering you to become an entrepreneur.

That voice of truth may be calling you out of a life of drugs and alcohol, and into community activism. That voice of truth may also be calling you to leave the comforts of a corporate job into full-time ministry. That voice of truth may be desperately calling you to escape a violent relationship. Whatever the voice of truth within you is calling you to become, it will not stop commanding, and it *will* win.

After he had spent so much time running from the voice and command of God to go to Ninevah, Jonah found himself in the lower chambers of a great ship, in the midst of a relentless storm, taking him in the opposite direction of God. After he realized he was causing more harm than he had intended to himself and others, Jonah confronted himself by asking, "Why am I wrestling against God?"

Instead of running from God sometimes just *being still* is moving us in the right direction towards Him. Resisting the urge to run can be a hard task. When we weigh the options, running most times can seem like the easy and painless escape. Those of us, who have endured the process of waiting on God, know all too well that the two words "*be still*" are much stronger than they sound to the human ear.

> But they that wait upon the LORD shall renew their strength; they shall mount up with wings as eagles; they shall run, and not be weary; and they shall walk, and not faint.
> (Isaiah 40:31 KJV)

When we face a crisis, we naturally see it as a bad situation. It takes us a moment to recognize the opportunity. We first encounter the attack. We feel struck and caught off guard when a crisis hits us. In mostly all disasters, we never have the chance to prepare for what is to come. Like an earthquake, it just happens. I want to think that this is God's way of getting us to see things from a new perspective. At the moment when tragedies occur, we cannot fathom how we will recover or make it out. So, here is where we ultimately are forced to fall on our knees and turn to God.

The people who have known me my entire life know that I have experienced the shock of crisis far too many times. I've encountered unexpected tragedy so many times that I began to wonder, "Will it ever end?" The crisis would come so often that I became my own enemy; killing my self-esteem with negative self-talk. I thought for a while, "This must be why I was born, to struggle." I thought, "Maybe it was meant to not be any better than this for me." I was tired of always feeling like I was in a war –in survival mode. I would entertain thoughts of suicide more times than most people would admit. When others would look at me and see strength, I could only stare in the mirror to see weakness and defeat. Still, my insecurities, fueled by lack and doubt, inevitably drew me closer and closer to the Father.

Each time as I endured the wrestling match with Him, I would find myself exhausted from the struggle and broken. Surprisingly to me, this was right where He wanted me. I found out that as long as I was wrestling and trying to work things out in my time and my strength (without God's help), I was going nowhere. I was merely running in circles. God would not allow my methods to work, because He had a plan. *God's plan* will always overpower *our plan*!

Before you attempt to work your way out of a bad situation, I encourage you to first consider His *grace*. I've faced countless tragic circumstances; some created by my own mistakes and misguided agendas. Surprisingly, each time I recognized that I was not in control. Each time, his grace would nt appear until I relinquished *my will* to Him.

Once as I was driving my children to church, I was pulled over by the police due to a traffic citation I had received months prior. Preoccupied with my responsibilities as a single mom, the court date disappeared from my radar, causing my driver's license to become suspended and a bench warrant had been issued.

Though I had intended to schedule time off work to resolve the matter on payday, my memory failed me and the authorities were there that day to remind me. Sitting in my car, devastated by the consequences and afraid of what my children would think of their mother, I held back my tears, as I felt I had finally failed them. This is not an image any mother would want her children to see; *mom in handcuffs like one of the bad guys*?

The moment the officer asked me to step out of the car I knew this was the beginnning of another defining moment in my life; as a woman, mother, leader, and minister. I knew there was no turning back. I had to go through the process. He could look in my face and see the fear and the tears I held back. So, he nicely offered to wait as I had a nearby friend to come and take my children and my car home as he gave me a *"courtesy ride"* to the *county hotel.*

As I sat in the *courtesy car*, the first thing I thought was, "It could have been worse." At that moment, I began to experience the grace of God. To most people, this would be a seemingly tragic situation. Once I surrendered to His sovereign will, in exchange I received the peace that comes only when you are certain that He is in control.

I sat in the holding room for about 5 hours as I arranged to pay the traffic ticket and be released. As I sat there still, my heart couldn't help but be moved with compassion for all of these women. They had all like myself, been exposed and rewarded with a courtesy ride to this county hotel. Contrary to the experience the enemy wanted me to have, I had tapped into *grace*. Would you believe me if I told you that His grace made my visit a delight?

Several women arrived in the holding cell, wailing in tears. As I sat there in stillness, silently holding on to grace, I couldn't help but ask God, "Show them, Your grace." One woman was inebriated and high on something. She was quite loud, cursing and beating on the windows. She walked over to me and asked aggressively, "Are you okay? Why are you just sitting there?" I didn't respond to her, but looking her in her eyes, I told that spirit where to go.

Another woman came in drowning in her tears –she cried uncontrollably. I asked the Father in prayer, "Show her your grace and release your peace." After I prayed for her, amazingly, she got down on the floor kneeling on the bench and began praying before God in

> *And He said unto me, My grace is sufficient for thee: for my strength is made perfect in weakness.*
>
> *(2 Corinthians 12:9 KJV)*

Spanish. She was still crying very hard, so I could not make out all that she was saying. However, I felt the presence of the Holy Spirit moving in the room. She didn't know it, but as she prayed, I agreed with her in the spirit silently. Eventually, she got up stretched out on the bench against the wall and went to sleep. In the midst of her storm, she went to sleep! That is the power of God's grace!

Another woman sat against the wall beside the door. Like several others, she cried the entire time I was there. Eventually, she came and sat beside me. She asked me, "Is this your first visit?" I told her yes. She looked at me in amazement as she says, "Wow, you are so calm!" and I replied, "It could be worse." She started sharing with me how she was in the car with her children as well. She felt like she had failed them. I encouraged her, "Seek the peace of God, He is with us here, and all is well. You will see your children again soon." She got on her knees and like the other woman she knelt at the bench beside me and began to pray silently.

When His grace appears, here is what it looks like: You will begin to try new ways of doing things that you might not have otherwise considered. People will offer to help you whom you may have otherwise dismissed. You discover unlocked doors that you didn't even know existed. Instead of you pacing the floor at night, wearing out the carpet with your tears, you will experience a sweet, peaceful sleep. Being able to sleep in the midst of tragedy is the most excellent example of peace that passes all understanding, the tranquility that cannot be explained with words.

Instead of sitting in a jail cell screaming and losing your mind, you will be able to sit still, listen for God's voice, and begin to share His grace with those who have never experienced it. You may want to tear the place up and give everyone who hurt you a piece of your mind. I can promise you that His grace will indeed keep you from losing it. No matter what situation you find yourself in, His grace will always meet you there. Keep in mind that God's grace is never rewarded to us because of anything we have done to earn it. We are never entitled to His grace. We have access to His grace for one reason alone:

His undying love for us. No matter how bad you might think you messed up, you can never exempt yourself from His love.

Once we allow our hearts to be softened and accept Gods will, we will enter God's grace, and begin to experience His rest. Then, we can be transformed by the renewing of our minds. When we can let go of our inhibitions and expectations, it becomes a pleasure to wake up each day and expect God's best to be done in our lives... *every day!* When we can let go of our *what-ifs* and *why not's*, we can begin to move forward with life as God intends it to be.

Jacob wrestled with the angel of the Lord and said, "I can't let you go until you bless me." He was doing all he could to protect his old identity. Jonah wrestled with God until he jumped off the ship and ended up in a whale's belly. He also did the best he could to hold on to whom he used to be. Jesus even wrestled with God in the Garden of Gethsemane. Until he finally said, "Nevertheless, not my will, but let Thy will be done." Now, as I add my name to the list, (feel free to add yours as well), I recognized that for over 30 years, I had wrestled with the path God chose for my life. Now that I have accepted His will (and bury the identity I created to survive) I can truly rest!

So, going forward (after hearing such an explicit command from the Father) I make a conscious effort each day to evaluate my environment. I assess my relationships, my agendas, and my goals. If I discover they were

167

created to protect the old me (old fears, old doubts, and old insecurities), I gladly let them go. I even evaluate my mistakes and shortcomings. If I can determine that they were meant to teach me a valuable lesson that I may one day share with another human being, I wouldn't dare look back in regret or feel devalued. I celebrate them!

We must learn to reconcile our paradigms with His, and that requires *stillness*. When we reflect on our darkest experiences, defeats, and failures, we must find a reason to celebrate them. When we arrive at a state of celebration, then we have discovered the rhythm by which we are supposed to move. Your "personal applause" demonstrates that you have replaced your perspective with God's perspective. Now you understand how even your most embarrassing moments were a part of His divine plan.

I am *becoming still* to feel the heartbeat and the pulse of God —so that my pulse matches His. I am *becoming still* so that my thoughts match His. I am resting; an act of surrendering my will and trading my desires for His. I am sitting still and waiting...I am letting God be God.

"Because of the extravagance of those revelations, and so I
wouldn't get a big head, I was given the gift of a handicap to
keep me in constant touch with my limitations. Satan's angel
did his best to get me down; what he in fact did was push me
to my knees. No danger then of walking around high and
mighty! At first, I didn't think of it as a gift and begged God
to remove it. Three times I did that, and then he told me, My
grace is enough; it's all you need. My strength comes into its
own in your weakness. Once I heard that I was glad to let it
happen. I quit focusing on the handicap and began appreciat-
ing the gift. It was a case of Christ's strength moving in on my
weakness. Now I take limitations in stride, and with good
cheer, these limitations that cut me down to size—abuse, ac-
cidents, opposition, bad breaks. I just let Christ
take over! And so the weaker I get, the stronger
I become."
(2 Corinthians 12:7-10 The Message Bible)

"As the deer pants for streams of water, so my soul pants for you, O God. My soul thirsts for God, for the living God. When can I go and meet with God?"
(Psalm42:1-2 NKJV)

THIRSTY FOR
LIVING WATER

"It's 6:30 am!" The alarm clock screams at us. "Don't you dare hit that snooze button one more time," my paycheck gently reminds me. Let go of the pillow and peel the sheets back. Is it Friday yet? NO. Take one deep breath and up on my feet. Make my way to the bathroom for the 1st trip of the day. This is that one moment of my day (which never lasts long enough) that I embrace the sweet silence. Then I hear the door down the hall, *"SLAM!"* One of the aliens *(teenagers)* is having a bad morning. Which is it; female hormones or male testosterone? I listen to each of their sad stories before releasing each dollar I possess to a last-minute worthy cause. I make sure the kids get on the bus safely and are dressed appropriately for the weather; pants aren't sagging, and jeans don't have holes. Did everybody get their homework done? What will I wear to work? I don't have time to iron. Holes in my hose? Oh well —no one can see them beneath my dress pants. Is there time for an egg or a muffin? Juice will have to do. Make sure I take something out for dinner. Chicken—one way or another. Where are my keys and my purse? Do I have gas in the car? I've got 15 minutes 'til time for me to clock in. Oh yeah, "By the way, thank you God for another day!"

"It's 5:00 pm!" My time card alerts me. Shut down the computer. Grab your keys and your coat. Make a beeline for the door and don't look back. If I could only make it to my car without being pulled into another phone call or email that needs my attention, then I will be another day closer to Friday. This time in my car is very sacred. It's the 45 minutes of peace between Job #1 and Job#2. Nobody is screaming, crying, or making demands of me. It's *MY TIME*! MY MUSIC! MY WAY! Make a quick stop at the store—sauce for the chicken and a pack of chocolate chip cookies for the kids. I pull into my driveway and prepare to clock in. I walk in the door *–six bags of groceries in tow*! Dropping my purse and the coat on the sofa only to reach for a pan, fill a pot with water, season the chicken, and slide it in the oven. I'm picking up toys, paper, and dirty socks on my way up the stairs. If I can just make it up to my room without one kid mischievously punching the other! Keep going; they're right behind me! I'm almost there! SLAM! Homerun! Touchdown! In my room, the door is shut, *and locked*!!

Everything in my hands fall to the floor. I fall on the bed and temporarily *EXHALE*. They begin to knock, "Can you please tell him to let me change the channel?" I finally whisper, "Thank you God for another day!"

Sound familiar? We wake up each day on autopilot rushing to complete our daily routines. We go about our lives from day to day with no thought of rest. Most of us have no idea how tired and empty we are until we are *forced* to be still. Many expect no more from life than the natural progression of school, college, marriage, jobs, raise the kids, and now more increasingly in our generation—*divorce*. Have we tragically grown accustomed and satisfied with this cycle? As we haphazardly complete the tasks at hand, we are growing emptier by the day. I am convinced that there is a small voice within each of us suggesting, "This can't be *it*!" We get up each morning, or come home after a long day's work—and as our heads fall in our hands during the silence of the day, we hear that voice within us crying out, "There has got to be more to my existence than this!" Allow me to introduce you to your *thirsty soul*.

Thirsty for Affection

Here she comes, approaching the well to draw fresh water. Exhausted from her journey. Tired from rejection. Weary from hoping that this moment or that moment will last a lifetime. She's told her girlfriends numerous times, "Oh how he loves me!" She is speaking of a new lover. Other times she has told people, "Oh how wonderful it is to know I have a real friend." She is speaking of someone who has come into her life –only to share a momentary bond. However, each of them (lovers and friends alike), like clockwork, find a way to disappoint her again.

Moreover, again, she is left with the cold silence of her own company. No one to swap jokes or share dreams. No one to cheer her on as she reaches for another star in the sky. No one to help her celebrate the "big win." So here she comes again, after giving the best of her soul to others who would not be there in the end. Here she comes back to the well; alone, ready to draw water. Surprisingly, this time she gets more than anticipated.

The woman at the well is always depicted as *thirsty*. She represents a mindset that we all identify with (male or female). We have all experienced the desire for life-long connectedness. Who hasn't at one time or another, experienced the anxiety associated with their search for that one person or thing that would satisfy this longing in their heart? The woman at the well is our demonstration of what it feels like to "long" for someone or something to come into our lives and fill the void of companionship.

As babies, we are fed constant affection from our parents, loved ones, and their friends. Then when we are children, our parents (if we are blessed to have them) pour out the affection we need. They pour out so much that we should never rely on security attachments from the world. As adolescents, and then as young adults, we begin to pull away from the security of our parents in exchange for the devotion of someone who will remain with us for a lifetime. That longing remains until we *hopefully* marry. Then, sadly, if we divorce we are sentenced back into the "longing line."

What we fail to realize is that starting from birth, we spend our lives craving security. We were detached from the ultimate form of security when we transitioned from eternity into time here on earth. That is the affection of our Heavenly Father. The bible says, "Before I formed you in your mother's womb, I knew you." (Jer. 1:5) He knew us in an intimate, loving and affectionate way; an association that cannot be replaced. Our birth parents, close friends, and spouses may attempt to emulate this affection. Still, similar to the woman at the well, we are all scheduled for a divine encounter with the Source. Until we make an authentic connection with the Father, our thirsty souls will return to the well longing to be replenished –again and *again*.

Until we recognize that what we are experiencing is a *spiritual* thirst, no other relationship we attempt to drink from will quench our thirst. Our spiritual appetites cannot be satisfied within the confines of connection with people. Our cravings will not be satisfied until we settle into a sacred and intimate love affair with Him. When we have craved authentic affection for a long period of time, we may find ourselves drawn to a hopeless desert. Sadly, as a result of the desert experience, we succumb to relationships that are not developed according to God's design. Women, we often close doors on relationships with our girlfriends once we no longer agree. Men also fall in and out of comradery as soon as they disagree with the fellas. Moreso, while we love our families (immediate and extended), these blood-borne relationships are not immune from becoming strained. Even family members experience the pain of disconnect when someone feels like you don't love them *the way family should.*

> *"But whoever drinks of the water I give him will never thirst. Indeed, the water I give him will become in him a spring of water welling up into eternal life"*
>
> *(John 4:14 NIV)*

The well she arrives at, Jacob's well –there is no water flowing freely –rushing in from a fresh spring. However, this well catches the dew and rain as it collects at the bottom. This reservoir becomes a well of water *that* will not flow. Jacob's well can be compared to our relationship wells. In comparison, our relationships may resemble this same stagnated trend. Many of our relationships lack the free-flowing affection we so desperately need. When was the last time you could honestly say you experienced a continuous flow of fresh affection rushing into your life?

To our surprise, we must learn that a fresh spring of affection would resemble: consistent, uninterrupted, intimate fellowship with Jesus Christ. The relationships we are seeking to fill our emptiness, are not satisfying our thirst –yet we continue to transition from one empty soul to the next; one failed relationship to another; one codependent friendship to another. They all have different names and faces –but flow from the same reservoir; each relationship encounter leads back to the same well, filled with lifeless *stillwater*. Sadly, each failed relationship leaves us emptier and thirstier than the last.

So here the woman is again at Jacob's well, looking for a drink. It's the middle of the day, so she doesn't have to worry about the traffic of others who come in the morning and evening. They know her story. They know her reputation. They even know how desperate she is. However, this time at noon, she's not at the well alone. Someone is there waiting for her –with an answer to a question that she hasn't asked. He is there waiting, ready to fill a void she didn't even know existed –*in her soul*.

She sees him there. Shockingly, the gentleman speaks to her first, asking for a drink of the water from Jacob's well. Here is Jesus, thirsty in his flesh. The woman who came prepared with her bucket to draw, she was thirsty in her spirit. He's looking past her mistakes, bad decisions, and shame. Even moreso, looking past her reputation and low self-esteem, he offers her a drink that would ultimately satisfy her thirst for affection. Today, at noon he would change her life altogether. He tells her in a nutshell, "Sweetie, if you knew the gift of God, and who I am, you would be asking *ME* for water. Then, I would freely give you some *living* water". He is such a gentleman –all you have to do is *ask*!

177

He goes further to warn her that, "As long as you are drinking, this water you will stay thirsty." As long as we remain in toxic relationships, we will remain thirsty. As long as we pressure people to give us the affection only God can bestow, we will overlook healthy relationships that were meant to last a lifetime. Still, there is an ultimate experience. When we learn to come to the well of living water to drink and be filled (and stop settling for the instant gratification found in still water) our longing will cease. God's love will draw us closer into His bosom and take us deeper in our relationship with him. Right there, in the heart of the Father, our appetite for affection is genuinely quenched.

Thirsty for Acceptance

There he sits, by the well. Fatigued and parched from his journey, Jesus gives us another example of thirst: *the thirst for acceptance.* Jesus stopped by Jacob's well while taking a break from training and baptizing the disciples. He was growing very popular—and very fast. The work of both he and John the Baptist caused Jesus to become a household name.

They diligently spread the message of the arrival of the Messiah; humanity had been eagerly waiting for centuries. Everyone, who had come to be baptized had embraced the practice of water baptism for the remission of sins. This new method of being cleansed from one's past sins was growing in popularity.

Here in this moment, Jesus was thirsty. In his human body, he was longing for water. The Jesus (the man) was tired. However, in his spirit, he was eager for the acceptance of mankind.

Jesus had the desire, given to him by the Father, for people to accept Him as "Christ." He was thirsty for someone to know *Him* from the inside out. He spent the last few years of his adult life, as it is written, preaching the gospel to unbelievers and craving for their acceptance of not only him; but also, the will of his Father. Always willing to serve and ready to show himself available, many times he found only rejection in return.

He was never selfish with the power of God inside of him. He never used his gifts to exalt himself. In fact, on one recorded occasion, Jesus told the man whom he healed to go on his way and not tell anyone about the miracle performed for him. The Messiah brought no glory to himself. You could depend on him to touch and impact your life, wherever it hurt. He would bring clarity wherever there was confusion. Wherever the sting of death emerged, he brought the joy of life.

Much like us, Jesus was a spirit on a human journey. He too experienced the hurt and loneliness that results from the constant rejection of those you love. One of the first places he went to perform miracles was his hometown; the place where everyone knew him. They knew whom he used to be, but could not fathom or embrace the power he now demonstrated. The Bible tells us that he went on his way and performed no miracles there.

On several occasions, we see Jesus steal away in the night to spend time alone with the Father. There, he didn't have to be the Messiah—*Savior of the world*. He could lay down his title. He could stop thinking about what everybody else needed. He could be Himself, just Jesus. Here, he could reveal his wounds and not be considered weak. Here he was not expected to be strong. He was accepted just as he was.

Here at the well, he would find a woman who would be not looking for healing. As she approached the well, he identified her cravings cleverly hidden beneath the surface. Surprisingly, when she arrived to draw from the well, she requested nothing. She didn't know his name. She'd heard nothing of his reputation. If he had not asked her for a drink, she would have habitually drawn her water and went about her way. Instead, an unexpected exchange took place. Jesus engaged her in a dialogue that would leave them both filled.

Upon hearing of his capacity to radically transform her life, the woman at the well quickly begged, "Give me this water, so that I won't have to be thirsty again." At that moment, she didn't see him as the Messiah. All she knew was he offered her something no one else had ever offered. Others offered temporary gratification, empty affections, and sometimes just plain sex. But here this unknown man, who seemed to know everything about her, offers so much more without asking anything in return. When he described the concept of living water to her, she didn't know anything about his title. She accepted him for who he was –the man who had manged to touch a placed in her heart that no one else knew existed.

How many times have we found ourselves longing for those who claim to know us, to get to know us on a deeper level—from the inside out? As leaders, we continuously pour ourselves out. Wherever we are needed we show up. On our jobs, we give of ourselves when others can't or won't deliver. For those who are financially successful, you meet the needs of relatives and friends in need, without expecting anything in return. Mothers nurture their children, tirelessly, from birth and even far into their adult years. Fathers surrender their lives to providing for their families; you go a distance no one else in the home is capable of going. Most single adults give tirelessly, just because everyone thinks, "They have no other responsibilities, so they should be able available."

Beyond all our giving, each of us has a desire for someone to know the real person hiding on the inside — not the *giver* or the *doer;* but the living, breathing, hurting individual. Many won't go the extra mile to cultivate an intimate relationship. It takes sincere interest to study a person. Those who need something *from us* are satisfied with whom they encounter on the surface, the representative. So as long as we are giving them what they need, it doesn't matter *what we need.*

Many spend several years in their marriage, feeling unaccepted. The most painful relationship to experience is that of a marriage where each spouse feels as if the other does not know him/her. You've said your vows, you loved the honeymoon, you bought the house, you raised the kids, and you got the promotion. Still, while completing this lifecycle, many couples never invest the time to study one another—from the inside out. For those that finally did, many didn't like what they saw.

After several years of marriage to my ex-husband, I finally asked the question, "Do you really love ME? Not the person you want me to be, but the person I am today? Not the beauty you see on the outside, but the Kimberly on the inside?" That day and his answer, for me, was the turning point in our relationship. I found out that his response was ultimately the source of the tears and loneliness I had been experiencing. Here I was, once again in my life facing rejection and disappointment. The relationship that was *supposed* to fill the void of companionship and last a lifetime would not last. Inevitably after divorce, I would find myself once again empty –craving a sense of belonging, affection, and acceptance.

The woman at the well told Jesus, "You have nothing to draw with, and the well is deep." In those times when the women drew water from the wells, it was common for them to use buckets to extract water and small wooden cups to drink. As noted earlier in this chapter, Jesus was thirsty for acceptance –that is what he expected to gain at the well. So, if he were going to obtain acceptance from the well how would he retrieve it?

God said, "If I be lifted up from the earth, I will draw all men unto me." (Jhn.12:32) In other words, when God becomes the origin of your efforts, He does all the persuading. Whatever we need from the well, He will draw it for us. Furthermore, when we exalt Him –acknowledging Him and making His ways supreme in all that we do –He will in return quench our thirst. He will fill us in the places where we are empty. No matter how desperate, empty or thirsty we become, there is no well too deep for the Father to draw from. For, He reaches down to the depths of our souls.

The acceptance Jesus craved was released from heaven as he (who was indeed God in life form) exalted the Father above his own mortal desires. See, as Jesus promised this woman that one day she would worship the Lord in spirit and truth, He lifted the Father. We must abandon our agendas so that the purposes of our heavenly Father are fulfilled. In doing so, we are lending ourselves to be used as His vessels; filling us with *living water*. It is in this manner that we are exalting Him above the earth.

He may then use us, His willing vessels, to pour out living water (by becoming living examples of His Spirit) and satisfy other thirsty souls; causing them to leave their wells of *stillwater (empty relationships)* altogether.

I must make a critical point here: Freedom is attractive. When we are free in our souls, others who *are not* can recognize the difference. They may not initially ask for a taste of the water we are drinking, but it is our job to offer it. God desires that we lend ourselves to His plan, becoming instrumental in leading others towards freedom. Then, He is *"lifted up"* (which means elevated above our human intelligence). The cycle never ends; He will continue to draw us closer to Him and replenish us with more living water.

I must warn you though—as the opportunity to demonstrate God's power increases in magnitude, the pressure for you to perform intensifies. However, in tandem, His exposure is magnified, and your potential for success becomes certain. Ultimately, the more He can draw from the well, then the more He can restore back into our empty tanks. It is a continuous steady flow.

The continuous flow looks something like this:

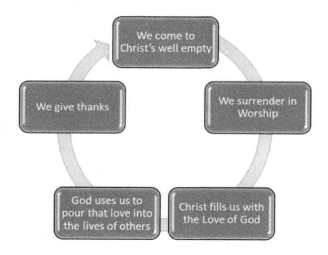

Thirsty for Accomplishment

"What does it profit a man to gain the world but lose his own soul?" *(Matt 16:26)* That is the question Jesus asks the disciples as he predicts his death at the cross. Here he is getting their minds wrapped around the idea that he hadn't come to use his reputation and power to become a celebrity. He would only give himself to the purpose God sent him to complete. If that one purpose were not accomplished, then his whole existence would have been in vain.

Paul encountered his season of desperation as he sat in multiple prison cells for numerous years. Paul of Tarsus was born with what was considered a rich man's citizenship. He was highly educated, extremely zealous, and articulate. He knew the law of the land, and he understood the bible like no other. He received the best training a Pharisee could receive. Paul worked hard and achieved the devoted status of Pharisee, who would go on to execute more Christians than anyone else. He had no reason to look down at those beneath his status quo or backward at those who had helped him to get where he was in life. He was a man who had accomplished the affection of his leaders and the acceptance of his peers. He was on his way somewhere in life. However, though Paul had gained the world, he was *losing his soul.*

Yes, he is on his way somewhere. However, here he is on the road to Damascus unaware that he is scheduled for a divine appointment with destiny; a meeting that would change the entire course of his life. This moment would discredit all the work he had done. It would also devalue the accolades, medals, and recognition he had collected for himself. This moment would destroy all of his networking efforts; he would now be forced to begin networking all over again.

He would be forced to build new relationships and generate a new following altogether. He would have to work hard to gain the affection and acceptance of a new audience all over again. Before now, Paul was consumed with a sense of accomplishment for his work. Others would give anything to have been in his position. Now, on this desert road to Damascus, He will know the thirst of accomplishment all over again.

In Genesis, we are told that we were "created in His image." Therefore, we are creators. Each day God was busy creating the heavens and the earth. At the end of each day, it was good, and He was successful. Then on the sixth day, He created us to bring Him glory for His work.

Like God, our Father, we wake up each day thirsty for success. Some of us look for the big win on our jobs by landing a major contract, resolving a significant conflict no one else could, saving the company a large amount of money, or getting a very long sought-after promotion or raise. Many successful business owners wake up each day, devoted to developing new cutting-edge business strategies and technologies. They work, day in and day out, with the hopes that their business will one day be a Fortune 500 company. Mothers who work in the home, work just as hard—starting each day with one success in mind, make everything in this home run smoothly for 24 hours.

If you recall from the intro-
duction of this book, when God
created humankind, He was
seeking glory for Himself – in
other words, "applause." Consider this: since we are *like Him*
we naturally seek applause for
our efforts as well. When the
promotion is announced, the
Fortune 500 Board sends out
the welcome letter, and the kids

*Pray also for me that
whenever I open my
mouth, words may be
given me so that I will
fearlessly make known
the mystery of the gos-
pel, for which I am an
ambassador in chains.
(Ephesians 6:20 NKJV)*

are all smiling in their beds, we then wonder, "Where is
the glory?" Who applauds our work? Who says well
done? "Does anyone even notice my victory?" Does it
even matter that I was born? When we hear no applause,
we make the mistake of thinking we haven't done enough
to deserve it. Moreover, as a result, we begin to run ourselves into the ground looking for the "BIG WIN" that
pushes us to the front of the crowd and demands the applause. We are thirsty for accomplishment.

One of Paul's most famous inspirations says, "For me
to live is Christ, and to die is gain." (Phil. 1:21) Little did
Paul know back on the Damascus road, his entire passion
for life would be re-routed. No longer would he spend his
life and use his efforts to gain the applause and recognition from man. Paul now craved a life of servitude that
might remotely imitate the life of Christ. This time he
would wind up having his parched desire for accomplishment quenched while sitting in a prison cell for the

remaining days of his life. To Paul the more he emulated the sufferings of Christ, the more significant he felt.

Paul now understood that his death would be more valuable than his life. He learned that to die and give his life to the works of Christ he will have accomplished much more than he ever could by gaining earthly rewards. He came to understand that physical rewards would have no value after death. However, to obtain an inheritance in Christ would cause him to reap an eternal reward. Paul was no longer thirsty for the applause of man; he would now gladly spend His days in a prison cell eager for the applause of Christ.

With the same level of passion that he gave to the works of the government, he showed that same fervor and devotion to the works of the gospel. Paul went on to write two-thirds of the new testament, mostly from his prison cells. Moreover, he continues to add millions of people to the faith today. Paul gave up the world, *but he gained His soul.*

Weary in the desert

So, by now you might be admitting to yourself, "I am in a desert, and I am thirsty." You might be saying, "I have traveled too far out to turn and go back the way I came. I can't change the events that brought me out to this dry place. My past is just what it is, *my past.* Now God, satisfy my thirsty soul in this dry and weary land. Give me this living water so that I won't know thirst again."

The second largest desert on the face of the Earth is the Sahara, in northern Africa. It comes second only to Antarctica stretching to over 3.6 million miles! The span of this desert is much too broad and hazardous for any person to travel on foot. An attempt to do so is indeed a death sentence. It is also the hottest desert recorded in history with temperatures reaching as high as 136 degrees Fahrenheit!

A desert is a perilous place. The air is dry, and the ground is hot. The atmosphere in the desert is so dry and hot that the body begins to lose water through sweat glands. Not many organisms can live or reproduce life while in the desert. This lack of production is because the soil is rocky, sandy, and dry, lacking the necessary minerals to produce. There is no sustenance found in the desert for living organisms to consume. Without water, any person or thing attempting to survive will ultimately die. To any organism subjected to the constant dry heat of the desert, water is a very vital but limited resource.

Our spiritual deserts resemble the Sahara, where we may encounter dire situations that are long, drawn out, or over-extended. Refuge may appear nowhere in sight. We sometimes go through long periods of heartache, pain, and discomfort. Our inability to cry or express our feelings may resemble the dry air of the Sahara; positioned underneath a cloudless sky that produces no rain.

Here in the desert, is where most people lose faith in God's promises and lose hope for rescue. After a couple of hours of exposure to the desert's sun and heat, we become delusional. All rationale goes out of the window as we seek to fill our thirsty souls. We are distracted from God, and we are now exerting all of our energy on survival. We started the journey coaching ourselves by saying, "Easy does it, one day at a time." We take each step and each breath with integrity and purpose. In the beginning, we are patient. We seem to have time for conversation with God on a regular basis. As time passes, our hope begins to fade. After weeks, months, and years of being in a desperate situation, it is natural to question the existence of God. You start to entertain the idea that somehow you have been fooled and have been left on this journey alone. That's when fear takes the stage.

Once we have succumbed to fear and doubt, the mirages appear. An illusion appears when the heat from the sun begins to hover and form waves in the air. If somebody is glaring at it from afar they will think what they see is water. Similarly, when we become spiritually delusional, we don't see people or things for who or what they indeed are.

We begin to imagine the things we want to see, instead of acknowledging the truth staring back at us. For example, if we meet someone while we are in a desert of loneliness, we may instantly think, "They are an answer from God. They have got to be the one!" If only you weren't so desperate for a sense of belonging, you would see the heartless snake instead. They are assigned to distract us, poison our thoughts, and chase us off course.

When we give in to temptation and settle for chasing the delusion, we are settling for less than the best that God has in store for us. Moreover, because we are distracted, in the end, we wind up rejected by the things and people we've mistaken for authentic, loving relationships.

It is critical to note that when you are in a spiritual desert, coyotes are lurking; watching and waiting for you to throw in the towel. They are waiting for you to faint in exasperation. They patiently wait until you give in to exhaustion. Spiritual coyotes wait for you to exhaust all of your ideas, and you no longer have the energy to fight off a predator. They cleverly disguise themselves as harmless. You never recognize their existence until you have given in. As soon as you surrender to the heat, they will come and easily claim their prey. Let's look at how much water scientists have determined our human bodies are composed of:

[11]*Up to 60% of the human body is water, the brain is composed of 70% water, and the lungs are nearly 90% water. Lean muscle tissue contains about 75% water by weight, as is the brain; body fat contains 10% water, and our bones*

---

[11] Source: http://ga.water.usgs.gov/edu/propertyyou.html "Up to 60% of the human body is water, the brain is composed of 70% water, and the lungs are nearly 90% water. Lean muscle tissue contains about 75% water by weight, as is the brain; body fat contains 10% water and bone has 22% water. About 83% of our blood is water, which helps digest our food, transport waste, and control body temperature. Each day humans must replace 2.4 litres of water, some through drinking and the rest taken by the body from the foods eaten."

carry 22% water. About 83% of our blood is water, which helps digest our food, transport waste, and control body temperature. Each day humans must replace 2.4 liters of water, some through drinking and the rest taken by the body from the foods eaten."

Isn't it interesting that though our bodies are made up of mostly water, we can still be in a state of *thirst*? We are walking reservoirs of water, but we can surely die of dehydration. Without continually being replenished we will find ourselves suffocating and drowning in our vessels. The same goes for our spirits. Many of us grew up in christian homes where the Bible was our blueprint for life. We can quote scripture and recite every religious cliché' in perfect timing. Still, many of us have struggled to find our way to a relationship with Jesus Christ.

A desert in the natural sense is a place that lacks precipitation. Rain is the only hope for survival. In a natural desert, rain comes very rarely. While on the other hand, in a spiritual desert, our lives are not so hopeless. The word *deserted* (which means: to be left alone) is derived from the word desert. In the natural sense, someone that is in a desert is considered to be 'alone.' Yet, Jesus reminds us that when we enter our spiritual deserts, he will never leave us nor forsake us. We are the bride, and He is the bridegroom. He has not *deserted* us.

When we remember that we are not alone, the desert is no longer a death sentence. Instead, our spiritual deserts have the capacity to be transformed into a place of harmony and peace. It is no longer a place of extreme

THIRSTY FOR LIVING WATER

drought. Instead, it becomes the place where we are drawn to find Him. We are compelled to approach the well of living water (Christ) and then invited to take a drink. While others observe us worshipping, in disbelief, we are no longer exasperated from the fight to survive. We are enjoying the relief found only in His presence.

Furthermore, we recognize that we are not giving in to the battle, but we are surrendering to Him. When we exalt Him (lift Him up, honor Him) in the desert, He will draw us closer to Him to drink. When we are weak, that is when He is strong. Right here is where we want to be, safe in His arms; not attempting to survive in our own strength, but ready to thrive by His spirit.

In Spirit

Jesus told the woman at the well that, "the hour is coming when true worshippers will worship him in spirit and in truth." I am convinced we are living in that very hour Jesus referenced. Our generation has faced countless tragedies and storms. Earthquakes, tsunamis, war, plagues, recession, and famine have tested the hearts of men, women, and children for ages. Our governments, domestic and abroad, have struggled to work together resolve the complex issues we face as one human race. Yet recently, the disasters are occurring more frequently, the damage is growing worse, and the death tolls continue to rise.

In a climate such as this world we live in today, prayer has become increasingly more popular. Increased prayer only happens when humanity finds itself positioned so that its intelligence and strength cannot resolve its problems. We are then provoked to summon the forces more powerful than our own.

> "But the hour is coming, and now is, when the true worshipers will worship the Father in spirit and truth; for the Father is seeking such to worship Him."
> (John 4:23 NKJV)

When we find ourselves wavering in the midst of a storm that we cannot control with our own two hands, we are forced to stretch them upwards towards mercy and grace. When we are tied to the tracks and see that the train is coming, we obviously need help. When we see no relief in sight, we thrust ourselves into our spirit form and call on a higher power that can perform above and beyond our natural abilities. Our ideas and ingenious minds won't protect us from destruction. Nor can our money and titles be a suitable lifeline. In this hour, the need for a closer relationship with God is revealed.

When we worship Him in spirit, we are engulfed in the amazement of the absolute power and presence of God. In order for us to recognize Him when we see Him, we must first acknowledge His Spirit. The more time we spend getting to know Him by the Spirit, it becomes much easier to recognize that *He is* Spirit. That Spirit is omnipotent—it is everywhere, at the same place and at the same time.

We each have access to the Father, through His Son and by His Spirit, whenever we need Him. Worship in the Spirit is an act of stepping outside of our natural existence and stepping into our original created form. Did you catch that?

Becoming authentic is the only way for us to find that place of stillness on the inside of us and enter into His presence. You don't need the help of any elements created by man. These are only by-products of spiritual worship. Gospel artists, musicians, authors, and speakers understand that this fundamental form of worship is vital. They understand that before they can get up to minister, speak, or play an instrument in such a way to compel others to worship they must first position themselves in stillness and quietness.

For our light affliction, which is but for a moment, is working for us a far more exceeding and eternal weight of glory.

(2Cor. 4:17NKJV)

Most people don't understand why many times ministry leaders must distance themselves from loved ones or temporarily isolate themselves from the crowd. God's chosen leaders understand that to minister in such a way that the audience can feel the wind of His presence, *they* must first spend time in His presence –in the spirit.

When we are in spirit form, we are not affected by the elements surrounding us. The river may be rising, but we are standing still. The lightning may be flashing, but we don't even blink. The thunder may be rolling, yet we are not trembling. Since we walk in the spirit, by recognizing that by faith we are capable of doing the unimaginable. It is possible for you to fix your spiritual eyes on His face and find affection, acceptance, and reward. Thus, when we are worshipping in the spirit nothing and no one can distract us from the mesmerizing sight of God.

It is painful to receive notice that the company you helped to thrive is now laying you off because of budget cuts. It is not easy to digest your house being foreclosed on, packing up your family and painfully pulling out of the driveway –away from the home you have created so many memories in. It is devastating to take your 9-yr old to the doctor for a routine examination, and within minutes be rushed to St. Jude's to find out that your child will spend the next 12 months in the hospital fighting to survive a battle with cancer. It is even more painful to get a phone call with the report that your 17-yr old son has hung himself in his bedroom after months of being on depression medication.

Many people turn to drugs, alcohol, and sex to find relief from the excruciating pains of life. Contrarily, as we take on the form of the spirit, we experience numbness to the pain that no pharmaceutical drug can provide. When we are in the Spirit, he (the Spirit) does all the work for us. When we feel suffocated and cannot breathe, he does the breathing for us. When we can't find the strength to get out of bed and get through another day, the Spirit will bring us to our feet. When we cannot find the words to say, the Spirit utters and groans the words for us. When the pain is just too much for us to bear, the Spirit becomes our undertaker, articulating a plea to encompass it all.

Moreover, in Truth

Jesus says, "True worshippers must worship in Spirit *and in truth.*" That means anything else is a waste of time and energy. Any other form of worship is counterfeit and bears no fruit whatsoever. For example, why would you pretend to be eating if there is no food? There must be substance when we worship.

Moreover, without the Spirit, we have no content with which to identify our worship. In that sense, we are only pretending

> If we claim to have fellowship with Him yet walk in the darkness, we lie and do not live by the truth.
>
> (1 John 1:6 NIV)

like little children dressing up for the school play. When the curtain closes and after they receive applause for their performance, the costumes are removed, and they are instantly transformed back to their reality: children. Contrarily, as we take on the form of the Spirit, we find the substance we need to keep going in the desert. We don't have to pretend to be surviving.

We don't have to dress up our issues and pretend they don't exist. Nobody gets to witness the power of God when we are only performing. However, as mature individuals we can drink from the well that never dries up, and thrive, even in the desert.

Our enemy would have us all to believe the lie that if our Father loved us, He would protect us from the dry, desert places in our lives. That same enemy taunted Jesus with this lie during his desert experience in the wilderness. This suggestion of God's negligence is absolutely not the truth. God sent His only son to die a bloody death at the cross. Even Jesus was not immune from pain and tragedy. The Father knew that this pain would be for his good.

Moreover, of course, in the end, it would not only be for Jesus' reward, but for ours as well. So, what makes you and I exempt? If you are going through a desert experience right now, ask yourself this, "Am I willing to accept the truth that this is actually for my good?"

When we worship in truth, we have accepted that nothing happens by accident or coincidence. It may seem that one lousy situation births another, and tragedy gives birth to destruction. It may appear as if every force of evil has been assigned to you alone. It may seem as if no one is traveling through the desert *but you*.

Consider this: lonliness is the only effective smokescreen the enemy can conjure up to distract you from the reality of your circumstances. I can assure you that each season of tragedy we enter is uniquely designed by our Creator, for our good. Paul said, "It was *good* that I was afflicted." Now, who in their right mind could face death head-on and make such a remark? Only someone who dares to worship the Lord in the *exclusiveness of truth*. Paul, like

Jesus, gave up his will *for God's will*. When he accepted the truth, that it indeed was good that somebody was willing to suffer, he then realized that his sufferings were not about him.

Paul came to understand that worship in truth is about *self-sacrifice*. When we can lay aside our agendas, and let go of our disappointments for somebody else to get a revelation about who God is, we are worshipping in truth. If we would stop protecting *our* image (and cease our worries about remaining relevant) a reflection of *Him* becomes visible. This level of emotional maturity is rarely demonstrated in our generation.

Most of us are addicted to what the media defines as success. We spend our lives working to emulate the images that we see in magazines, television, and radio. We work and run like horses; so laborious to the point that we are too tired to enjoy the fruits of our labor. We spend enough money on self-preservation that could potentially end world hunger. We are spinning our wheels backward, and going in the opposite direction of the abundant life we are trying to reach. Our generation is overly willing to sacrifice the gift of a harmonious life, for the sake of an *image* of success.

Worship is not only sitting still and being quiet in His presence. Worship is apparent when we examine the way we endure the weary aspects of our existence. When we go through the desert thirsty and exhausted, how we respond to the situation can be defined as worship. When we smile and make peace with our enemies –we are worshipping. When we wake up rejoicing, the morning after our car just got repossessed —we are worshipping. When we can sing and dance at the funeral of our loved ones – that is *indeed* worshipping. Authentic worship is not only found in being still. Worship is also demonstrated as we decide to charge against the wind and paddle against the current of life.

Living Water

The loss of a spouse, divorce, rejection by family, and lack of inclusion by society are all ways in which we enter our spiritual droughts. Many times, we search to have our emptiness filled through relationships with others. While Jesus clearly advised us to love one another, he never intended for us to substitute God's love with the love of man. Since we are so empty and the void is so painful, we sometimes settle for anything that resembles love. As a result, we end up in unhealthy relationships, love affairs, or toxic friendships. When those relationships fail us, we find ourselves hurt, frustrated, and emptier than we began.

Many times, we seek to have that emptiness filled with a sense of accomplishment. At one point in my life, I had a strong desire to reach the top of the corporate ladder. Later on, I discovered that I was looking for a '*sense*' of accomplishment. I realized that if I didn't stop the climbing soon, I would find myself at the top, still alone. When you find yourself in the desert of rejection, it's quite easy to subscribe to the idea that if you accomplished something great you will be accepted. You begin to believe the lie, that says you must qualify for love by performing and achieving success. I had experienced an unbelievable measure of rejection in my life. As a child, I felt rejection from my mother, I searched for acceptance within my extended family, and for over 40 years had never identified my biological father. When I did finally identify with who he was, again I achingly discovered even more rejection.

So, I spent 40 years transitioning from one relationship to another, yearning to discover my significance in somebody else's life. I wanted to prove to the world, myself included, that I was somebody special. The dilemma here is that I allowed the pain I felt from rejection to push me further away from God –instead of drawing me near to Him to be filled. I was in a thirsty pursuit of accomplishment when I really should have been in search of Him. After making some changes to my way of thinking, I soon began to recognize something new. I recognized that, I must become consumed with the Spirit of God in me to experience my life as a satisfied soul. As I began to pursue Him, in worship, the accomplishment eventually began to chase after me.

Our human instincts will compel us to fear; to chase the people and things that bring us instant gratification. When you have been in a drought, temporary relief is much more attractive than a season of perseverance. Whether you are seeking relief from loneliness, rejection, or just your inadequacies –the living water that Jesus offers us is much more effective and filling. No empty marriage, sweaty affair, or publicized accomplishment can satisfy your thirst for Him. They are only placeholders for the real thing. Things and accolades can never present real satisfaction – only a superficial and temporal identity of joy. Once you have pursued and obtained these placeholders, you will only find yourself *still thirsty*.

The Bible tells us that, "The latter rain shall be greater than the former rain." (Joel 2:23) Between the seasons of former rain and the latter rain, there lies a desert. That desert is the place where we learn to cultivate worship. During this desert experience, we are challenged to examine our faith and our capacity to endure pain.

Many do not survive their desert experience. Some are never able to conjure up the endurance required to advance to the other side. Yet, so many others find out that there is a well with free-flowing water, right on the inside of us. We can come as often as we please. We can drink and experience satisfaction.

However, the only way to tap into this reservoir is to worship. I do not mean you are restricted to worship in the traditional sense; hands raised and dancing to the tunes of modern day gospel. Surrendering our bodies to the sound and rhythm of music will enhance our time in worship. Still, authentic worship takes place when it is not provoked by music, the church praise team, or walking in the church at all.

Real worship can take place by just taking a walk in the park and enjoying the elements of God's creation; water, land, and air. Each time you inhale a deep breath you are breathing Him in. Real worship can take place as you adore Him in the absence of the crowd. Real worship can take place by sitting still on your back porch at night counting the stars. Real worship takes place when you can remove yourself from the emotional desert you are in and place yourself in His presence. When you can stop focusing on all that is going on around you and engulf yourself in His love –that's when real worship takes place. Real worship occurs when we worship in the manner as Jesus spoke, "*in Spirit and in Truth.*"

Once we drink from the well of living water Jesus spoke of, it will be impossible to drink from any other well and be filled. It just does not taste the same. The freshness and purity of living water cannot be replicated. Yes, the *latter rain* is more considerable, but only because it is produced after the desert experience; after we have discovered our ability to be filled with the living water that comes as a by-product of our relationship with Jesus Christ. The latter rain is more exceptional because we no longer have to wait for others to pour into us. It has begun to flow freely from within us.

The manifestation of the latter rain does not signify an absence of future trouble. However, it is our assurance that we will never go thirsty again. Newsflash: You are not thirsty for affection, acceptance, or accomplishment. Your mind, body, and soul are desperate for water that produces sustainable satisfaction. You are thirsty for water that is alive and can perpetuate an abundance of life. Come to the river that never stops flowing. Drink and be filled. You'll find the life you've been craving—*right here at the well*.

"*I long to drink of you, O God, drinking deeply from the streams of pleasure flowing from your presence. My Longings overwhelm me for more of you! My Soul thirsts, pants, and longs for the living God. I want to come and see the face of God.*"
(*Psalm 42:102 TPT*)

Rivers of living water shall
flow from within the hearts of
those that believe.
(John 7:38)

THIS TREASURE

"Step right up! Come one! Come all! Enter in at the gate!" the guard standing near gate shouts to the crowd. He continues, "Thirsty souls must enter at the gate, and come into the outer court. Spiritual cleansing begins here." There are so many standing near the entrance. But they stagger as they seem to be indecisive about entering in. Don't they know that this is the *great beginning*? This is the answer they have all traveled so far and for so long to find. But as I watch them stumble blindly around the gate, it amazes me that so many people could be standing in the presence of water but prefer to remain thirsty. I admit the gate is huge and quite intimidating; radiating its preeminence. The gate is absolutely beautiful! One can't help but to wonder if the gate alone is that beautiful, just how much splendor must await on the other side. But, I'm not like the others, I refuse to turn back in fear. I'm just so thirsty! My mouth is parched, and my soul is dry within me. My back and shoulders feel heavy as if I am carrying bricks. My hands and feet are dry, hard, and tired. Many of my friends and loved ones have deserted me along the way. Each time I thought someone had come along to take the journey with me, help me carry the load, they only walked away –taking some of me with them. But I kept moving forward. *Something* pushed me here. I've cried until my eyes have emptied their tears. *Something* wouldn't let me quit. When I wanted to give up and go back, *something* had a firm hold of me. With every sigh along the way its grip only grew stronger. As I wrestled to hold on to the things that made me feel secure, a whisper in the wind said, "Let it go." *Something* wonderful drew me here. If I can just press past the crowd, I'll make my way in. This time no one is going to stop me. This time, no one will talk me out of my decision to take a drink and be transformed into the woman I knew I could become. Grasping the courage to abandon my complacencies, I made it all the way here alone. I've traveled so far away from the safety of the walls built up around me; I simply cannot turn back now. My hands have been clinched tight this entire journey, but now my fingers are released, and

> *Open to me the gates of righteousness, I will go through them, And I will praise the Lord. This is the gate of the Lord, through which the righteous shall enter.*
>
> *(Psalm 118:19-20 NKJV)*

206

they're relaxed. I'm standing in the doorway, my broken heart skips a beat, and I gasp for air to breathe. In an instant, the one step which took me a lifetime to find the confidence to attempt, it happens. As I cross the threshold of deliverance, the forces that have fought for so long to hold me captive to fear and shame –they finally lose their grip. Like a pole vaulter running with her pole in hand, plants it for the catapult, and then releases it for her body to be thrust across the high bar for victory –I emerge beyond the gate. Relieved and exhaling after my flight, I manage to raise my tired arms in rejoice. My heart begins to sing a new song,

"Yes! I made it in.
I'm free from my sin and shame,
I see, and now I believe!
I'll never be the same!"

In case you weren't aware, this resembles the journey many of us have traveled as we worked our way towards accepting Jesus as Saviour of our lives. Tired from the journey, we find ourselves at the gate of God's heart; hoping to make our way in and at last find home –the place where we are promised a haven of peace and rest. Sadly, still, many arrive at The Gate and remain paralyzed there, at The Gate; unsure of what lies on the other side. So, they never enter in and experience the fullness of His presence.

However, like you and I, many refuse to travel this far in their lives and not receive the promise. We have suffered, sacrificed, and given up so much. We bit our tongues and gave up our rights to remain humble. We've been falsely accused, our love rejected, and our testimony scorned. Bewilderingly, we remember that there is a living promise. There is a reward, and we are *ready* to cash in.

We have spent countless years wrestling to relinquish our will. So as we enter beyond the gate, we find ourselves led first to the *Brazen Altar* (the furnace of extraction). It is a fiery furnace where the identity we were using all these years is burned up and utterly destroyed.

By entering this relationship with God, we have chosen to accept a new identity. We are no longer our own. Our friends on the outside thought we were crazy, so they left us to finish the journey alone. Still, our decision to travel beyond the gate must always be examined in this furnace first.

Once we decide to go the full distance to complete God's cycle of change, we should not be surprised when our lives are thrust into a season of unwarranted challenges. While it is commendable that you have declared with your mouth that you will by any means necessary turn over a new leaf, it is the Master's duty to have you examine your own decision.

Here at the furnace, He is asking us, "Do you really believe? Do you really want to change? Have you counted the full cost of the process? Are you ready to have your heart broken by lifelong friends and family members? Can you handle the pressure? Are you really ready?"

Before you go any further, it is critical that you have no one else to point the finger at and say, "I was misled." Before you take another step in your process of recovery, you will undoubtedly understand your decision and who/ what you are walking away from.

In this temporal furnace, the image we have worked so hard to create is consumed by the fire of His love, and discarded. As a result, we emerge with the model we began with: *His* image. Here, we have no comrades, constituents, or confidants. We have no titles or accomplishments to magnify our existence. During the test, we try to conceal our loneliness with church involvement, work, public achievements, and busyness. We begin to question ourselves, "Did I really make the right choice?"

For you formed my inward parts; You covered me in my mother's womb. I will praise You for I am fearfully and wonderfully made; marvelous are your works, and that my soul knows very well. My frame was not hidden from You when I was made in secret, and skillfully wrought in the lowest parts of the earth. Your eyes saw my substance, being yet unformed. And in your book they were all written, the days fashioned for me, when as yet there were none of them.
(Psalm 139:13-16)

Just as we begin to wonder, we are lead towards the water to be replenished; consequently, leaving the altar naked and unashamed. Our thirsty souls are escorted to the *brazen lavar* (a basin or tub) to wash. You have advanced beyond the fire of His correction. The smoke and ashes are about to be washed away.

In case you weren't aware, the brazen lavar is crafted out of bronze mirrors, used by Israelite women. Therefore, when you look into the basin ready to be refreshed, you immediately see a reflection. The reflection you see is a clearer perspective of how God sees you. Before you entered in at the gate, you saw one image in the mirror. However, similar to the way He could look beneath the oceans and see a treasure lying beneath—God is looking beneath the surface of your disguises and He sees a different model. He looks beyond what we see with our natural sight.

He sends us to the brazen altar to burn off (*unmask*) the reflection (*mindsets, attitudes, desires, mannerisms*) of the world with which we have learned to identify. All of us detached from our Heavenly Father, are born in search of acceptance and inclusion. We have this innate desire to "belong", to be chosen, to be desired. Sadly, as a result, we have become conditioned to behave and perform in ways which are acceptable by society.

Now, God wants us to see ourselves as He sees us. He wants us to identify with the authentic beauty and glory He created in us. When you gaze in the mirror, He doesn't want you to see a reproduction of the superficial images exhorted on social media or television. Our Creator desires that we recognize *His* masterpiece. You are radiant and beautiful in His eyes. Until we start to identify with all that He is, and that all of His splendor is infused within us, He cannot begin to quench our thirsty souls.

When will you start believing what God spoke about you? God has told us in His word many times how much He loves us and how much we mean to Him. Even the angels look upon us and wonder, "What is man that You are so mindful of him?" (Psalms.8:4-8) Rather, somehow, we tend to keep forgetting. We fall in our valleys and forget that we are royalty. Still, He promises us a future filled with rewards in exchange for our obedience and sacrifice to do things His way.

Once we look in the mirror and begin to see what He sees, then we can believe what He says. As a very young lady, my self-esteem was very low, and I had begun to believe the lie that I was not valuable enough to be considered precious. I had no idea how "*rare*" I was. I couldn't begin to fathom that I was *born* qualified to live a *rich* life –filled with God's adoration. Though I was born into a life deemed by society as poverty, it would take me decades to discover that I had been indeed *born rich*.

Born to a single mother, I had no idea what functional resembled. Then, during my adolescent years, I was moved from one relative's or friends home to the next. Given the instability of my childhood, I found myself in one relationship after the next; subjecting myself to rejection and abuse.

The painful cycle would only repeat itself over and over again. I'd cling to friends (and lovers) thinking I had to hold on to bad relationships; even if I only experienced a mere fraction of what I thought was love. Typically, I believed that fraction was all I'd ever receive.

Most times I knew the person didn't genuinely love me or even like me. Still, hopeless and vulnerable, I *held on*. Not knowing that I was strong enough to stand tall on my own two feet, I *held on*. Not knowing the warrior on the inside of me existed, I *held on*. Not knowing that I was indeed royalty, I *held on*. Not believing "anyone else" would think I deserved better, I repeatedly settled for the fractions, and *held on*.

If anyone had told me back then, that I was not at all the worthless, shameful little girl, I was conditioned to believe I was –but instead a successful author and a minister of the gospel –I would not have perceived it. If you had told me back then that God had chosen me, of all people, for the great assignment of reaching the lost, broken, and hurting, I would have told you to check what you were smoking.

However, my heart and my mind have been made pure and whole again by the power of His word at the brazen altar. Now, I see what He sees. I no longer view life peering through the eyes of abuse. I don't see the rape. My confidence is not interrupted by the deception and shame of sin. My perspective is not distorted by fat or skinny. My future is not determined by rich or poor. My thoughts aren't hazed by cloudy smokescreens of depression. Furthermore, I am no longer conditioned to make decisions based the paradigms my enemies have projected for me.

Instead, I can see a clear reflection of the King. As I glance in the mirror, I pause. My eyes are gleaming as I stare in the face of royalty. I see His beauty resonating from within me, and now I believe the report of the Lord. I was purchased out of a slavery mentality at a very high price; a cost so expensive that only the blood of His Son could satisfy.

Change begins with a thought. If you are never challenged in your thinking to imagine beyond your expectations, the process of change will never commence. Once you are introduced to a new way of thinking, here is what happens next: your loyalty to that paradigm will be challenged. If you *endure* to the end, that challenge will prove to be life-altering.

Most times when you detect a drastic and authentic change in someone, rest assured, their change started on the inside long before you could witness it on the surface. When we align our inner conversations with what God says about us, then, an exchange begins to take place. He takes your shame and hands you value and self-worth in return. He takes the tears you have cried at night and in return hands you the joy that comes from knowing you are not alone. He takes your feelings of worthlessness and hands you validation in its place. He removes your rejection and abandonment issues and hands you a birth certificate with the Father's name box filled in "Abba" which means Father! He created you on purpose and with purpose. When you become consumed with what

God says about you, His love and power intensifies within you –and an infectious form of joy and confidence exudes from you.

Haven't I commanded you? Strength! Courage! Don't be timid; don't get discouraged. God, your God, is with you every step you take."
(Joshua 1:9 The MSG Bible)

I grew tired of hearing the voice of royalty inside of me begging, pleading, and shouting to be set free. Soon, I found myself going after God with everything I had. Thirsty for a real experience of love and intimacy, I let go of every co-dependent relationship I had been in and ran to the well of living water. I began to drink from His fountain of love.

Some thought I was becoming arrogant, being funny, or just trippin' again. However, that wasn't the case. I just no longer felt dependent upon them to satisfy my cravings for affection. I don't mean in the sense that I wanted to be on an island of solitude. Rather, I no longer saw myself as a fraction of what I could be. I began to enter wholeness.

I got excited about dressing up and requesting a table for one or one ticket to the show. Everything and everyone else I had put my hope in had disappointed me one way or the other. So, I had nothing left to lose. Finally, I surrendered all. I said, "God take the house, take the car, take the husband...take it all. Have your way, Lord. But, just *help me to break...FREE!*"

Where is your confidence?

When you are sure about a thing, you are bold in your presentation of it. Furthermore, when you have tangible evidence that something exists, your confidence is not tested. For example, when you get ready to sit down, naturally you turn

> *"Being confident of this very thing, that He which hath begun a good work in you shall perform it until the day of Jesus Christ"*
>
> *(Philippians 1:6 KJV)*

around and look for the chair. Seeing it there, at your pleasure you sit and find rest. No one squats and bends down to sit *hoping* that there is a seat to catch them. However, if you did, that would be a real demonstration of faith. You haven't looked therefore you have no evidence that it exists. (Go ahead and try it. I can assure you that you will quickly discover the sheer magnitude of confidence you really possess!)

[12]Merriam Webster's Dictionary states that, *confidence* is, "a. a feeling or consciousness of one's powers, *and* b.the quality or state of being certain". The first definition does not merely refer to one's power absent of God. It does, however, refer to the power which was invested in us by the Holy Spirit. That power is a gift. When we were formed, we were created in His image (Gen 1:26-27). When you consider the image of God, you are forced to see Him as powerful, creative, and authoritative. He can

---

[12] Source: https://www.merriam-webster.com/dictionary/confidence

make mountains move at the sound of His voice. He created a vast ocean and millions of miles of dry ground without breaking a sweat. He placed the sun, moon, and stars in the sky and produced an award-winning daily performance. He parted the Red Sea with a single breath. God set the children of Israel free after 400 years of slavery. Then He did it again many moons later when he abolished slavery in America.

Now consider this: He thought so much of you and me, that He decided to deposit in us that very same power. Yes! It's in you too!

Adam and Eve sinned in the garden of Eden. Consequently, we were all perpetually disconnected from the power of God. When Jesus stepped foot on this Earth, His supreme goal was to reconnect us back to the power of God; the very same power granted during creation. Yes, it was always in us (lying dormant), but we were no longer *conscious* of it.

We were told to work and survive by the sweat of our brow. Hence, we could only trust that God still loved us enough to provide for us. When we did things that were not pleasing to God, our only resolve was to present a burnt sacrifice to Him, hoping for forgiveness. Notice I didn't say believing –but hoping. Let me ask you this: What good is 'hope' if you have no 'belief'?

Then, Jesus came and lived out a demonstration of excellence –as a mere mortal man. The Bible records his life experiences, subject to all the same emotions and anxieties as other humans. However, even though He was subject to the same temptation for sin, he remained humble and righteous in his responses; disturbing those who were supposed to be leaders.

Though he grew tired, hungry, and cold, He demonstrated the ability to endure the direst circumstances with grace. He gave himself in service when He was tired. He fed others when the pantry was bare. He calmed others when they were afraid in the storm and charged peace to "Be still." Moreover, he allowed himself to be beaten, scorned, and cheated out of life.

Newsflash! Jesus was not killed –he died! There is a difference. Being confident of the power that was in Him, and certain of the outcome, he was able to lay his life down for each of us. He allowed himself to be nailed and hung on a cross –dying for the redemption of the very ones who put him there. He came to show us who we really are and gave us the evidence we needed to be convinced. Jesus is our evidence. He came as an alarm – announcing the existence of God's power that lies in us. He came to make us confident!

You might not always *feel* the power, because it is intangible. I, therefore, challenge you to remain *conscious* of it. As long as you are aware of it, then no matter what mountain you face, you will be *confident* that there is something in you to assist. There is a force within each of us that will seem to manifest in the face of adversity. That power is what will carry you into grace. When the odds are stacked against you –and you realize there is no one to call on, you will be forced to reach for something or someone higher and more significant than what you see in the natural.

When the children of Israel left Egypt, they soon faced their moment of manifested confidence. As they stood on the shore with their faces toward the sea, knowing Pharoah and his army were bringing certain death behind them, they were forced to make a choice. They were forced to choose between believing that their victory was a joke and having the confidence to move forward.

We know how the story ends; the Israelites decided to employ their belief in the great "I AM". They chose to believe that the God who had spared the lives of their firstborn children, and led them out of 400 years of dogmatic and inhumane slavery, would not have brought them out to destroy them here. They chose to have confidence in their future. Here they decided that "though there was stability back there, I won't go back to the way things used to be." They decided, "I won't go back to slavery, I will embrace the freedom ahead of me."

Since they were in slavery for so many years, none of those standing at the sea even knew what "freedom" was. They had no idea what it meant to provide or think for themselves. They had no idea what it meant to wake up each morning and make a conscious decision on how to spend the day. They had no understanding of what it meant to be "free to worship." Every decision regarding their existence was made on their behalf. The only life they understood was that of a slave.

Here, watching the hand of God split and peel back the ocean like a banana, and stepping onto dry ground, they see God reward their confidence in Him. Moreover, here they find out just how much God loves them. Here, they received their reward for demonstrating the courage to rely solely upon His love for them.

But we have this treasure in earthen vessels, that the excellency of power may be of God and not of us.

(2Corinthians 4:7)

If we are confident of nothing else, we must grow to the place where we remain firmly secured in His love for us. However we experience life, and wherever we find ourselves –whether facing an army of enemies coming to attack us or finding ourselves in a desperate desert of abandonment—if we will habitually reach inwards and connect with the unconditional love God has for us, then we will come through our adversities like champions each time. When you are absolutely convinced and conscious of His Love, which is in you, you are always a champion! You have searched and found the treasure that so many spend their whole lives seeking *–His love in you.* God's passion for you is the fountain of living water that continues to flow even in a desert. That love is the "treasure in earthen vessels" that Paul referenced. He even went so far as to tell us, "If I have not love I am nothing." (*1 Cor 13:2*)

Hear this, "The attack and the dark season came because God assigned it." It is no news to God that you are

219

in or entering a storm. He formed it. So, brace yourselves, and be confident!

Paul tells us that, "All things work together for the good, to them that love God." (Rom. 8:28) Many hear and quote that scripture without taking note of the fact that the 'things' Paul referred to were hardships. It might be easier to capture the thought if he had merely stated, "*all hardships work.*" However, know this, depending on how you perceive them, all hardships indeed have the propensity to reverse your perspective. Everything may look upside down and sideways in your life right now. The pain and the pressure may not feel too delightful. The fear that haunts you at night may be inconvenient. Yet, while you're enduring, when you least expect Him to arrive – God will come through and reveal why He took you down this path. You'll be amazed and in awe when it becomes clear that it was indeed 'for your good'.

Confidence is not only used to get a light bill paid or saving your car from the repo man. Confidence is exhibited by believing God for a miracle when the doctor tells you that you have entered stage four cancer. We witness confidence in the bravery of our young men and women who enlist to the armed forces when the probability of war is elevated. As parents, we see the threat of death. Instead, they see an opportunity to make a difference in the world.

We see confidence when a young man looks in his child's eyes, as he wheels him through the hospital into chemotherapy. We see confidence as that father looks in his eyes and persuades him to believe that everything is going to be okay –even though the doctor has already advised him his son has only a 20% chance of survival.

We observe confidence in the face of a man on the day he discovers he's being laid off from work. The wife and the kids have no idea it has happened yet. Still, he prepares himself to deliver them a message of hope in the face of uncertainty. When he walks through the door, they see confidence.

We recognize confidence in the face of a mother after her husband abandons the family –leaving her to feed and raise seven children in the middle of a recession. She rises to the occasion, squares her shoulders, and does whatever it takes to get them all off to a good start in life with limited resources. One by, they emerge from their upbringing as productive citizens, and call her blessed!

Women who pack bags in the middle of the night to escape an abusive relationship are demonstrating confidence. She's been beaten, and so many times she has come within an inch of the end of her life. Ashamed, no job, and nowhere to turn, she shows up at the doorstep of a shelter looking for answers and a new start.

We identify confidence when a teenager arises from their sleep each morning, looks themselves in the mirror, and then heads off to school. Each morning they head off knowing that again today they will be taunted and bullied because of the color of their skin, their religious differences, the length of their hair, or the way they dress. We celebrate confidence when those same children share the gospel of Jesus Christ to another student while sitting in the library, on the playground, or in the cafeteria.

The opportunity to exhibit confidence arrives in a myriad of diverse circumstances. If you haven't had an occasion lately, fear not. We all have an equal opportunity to encounter storms. We are challenged each day to "Be strong in the Lord, and in the power of His might!" Jesus made it clear to us that we will experience hard times as long as we are living. He also dealt us a promise of hope and a charge to *be confident*. Know this: as long as we firmly cling to His promise of HOPE –we have nothing to fear my dear readers. Jesus has already overcome the world.

"Be strong. Take courage. Don't be intimidated. Don't give them a second thought because God, your God, is striding ahead of you. He's right there with you. He won't let you down; he won't leave you."
(Deuteronomy 31:6 The Message Bible)

OTHER GREAT BOOKS
BY KIMBERLY MICHELLE FORD

THE CORE
It's All Inside ! ! !
Find it at www.Amazon.com

HOPE FOR THE SOUL
Make Yourself at Home
In God's Heart
Find it at www.Amazon.com

Share your reading experience !
Will you help me to be a blessing to others ?
Please leaving a favorable book review on
www.*Amazon.com*.

ABOUT THE AUTHOR

*M*inister Kimberly Michelle Ford, a native of Atlanta Georgia, has committed her life to helping individuals heal and recover from abuse. She is committed to teaching survivors how to maintain a life of freedom as a result of her own personal experience with sexual and domestic abuse. In 2007, Kimberly released her autobiography, "The Core: It's All Inside." In her first book, she ministers to men and women alike who have suffered from the effects of sexual abuse, domestic violence, homelessness, and absentee parents.

She recognizes that these are issues that far too many of us have encountered. In 2017, she founded the Freedom Soul Foundation, LLC. to promote Domestic Violence awareness, support, and recovery. The foundation's mission is to enrich the lives of domestic violence survivors and victims' families. Under her leadership, the foundation works to erase the negative stigma associated with speaking out by applauding and rewarding survivors who have exhibited the courage to LIVE. Kimberly Ford is passionate about empowering survivors to live a life of continued freedom from abuse. "Being an advocate for others is not just about helping them to *get free*. Concurrently, advocacy involves teaching individuals how to *stay free*. I pray that as a result of my courage to walk in total freedom, others are inspired to pursue freedom too!"

~*Kimberly Michelle*

CONNECT WITH ME

Visit my website @ www.kimberlymichelleford.com
Or, @ www.freedomsoul.org
ITUNES Podcast @ The FreedomSoul Sessions
INSTAGRAM @ Kimberly.Michelle.Ford
FACEBOOK @ KimberlyMichelle

55004425R00127

Made in the USA
Columbia, SC
08 April 2019